CONGREGATION
FOR INSTITUTES OF CONSECRATED LIFE
AND SOCIETIES OF APOSTOLIC LIFE

THE GIFT OF FIDELITY
THE JOY OF PERSEVERANCE

Manete in dilectione mea (*Jn* 15:9)

GUIDELINES

LIBRERIA
EDITRICE
VATICANA

On the cover:
For you, Lord, give light to my lamp;
my God brightens my darkness (*Ps* 17:29)
Byzantine light, Jerusalem (4th century)
© Photo: Sr. Maria Smoleń, fmm

Print on Demand Edition 2021

© 2020 – Amministrazione del Patrimonio
　　　　　della Sede Apostolica e Libreria Editrice Vaticana
　　　　　Città del Vaticano – All rights reserved
　　　　　International Copyright handled by
　　　　　Libreria Editrice Vaticana
　　　　　00120 Città del Vaticano
　　　　　Tel. 06.698.45780
　　　　　E-mail: commerciale.lev@spc.va

ISBN 978-88-266-0644-6
www.libreriaeditricevaticana.va

Introduction

1. Our time is a time of trial: "it is more difficult to live as a consecrated person in today's world."[1] The struggle for fidelity and the lack of strength to persevere are experiences which belong to the history of religious and consecrated life since its beginnings. Fidelity, despite the eclipse of this virtue in our time, is engraved in the profound identity of the vocation of consecrated persons: it has to do with the meaning of our life before God and the Church.[2] Coherent fidelity enables us to grasp and reclaim the truth of our own being, that is, to *remain* (cf. *Jn* 15:9) in God's love.

We are aware that today's culture of the provisional influences our life choices, and the

---

[1] FRANCIS, *The Strength of a Vocation, A Conversation with Fernando Prado*, USCCB, 2018, Washington, DC, pg. 39.

[2] Cf. FRANCIS, Apostolic Exhortation *Gaudete et exsultate,* (March 19, 2018), 170.

very vocation to consecrated life. This culture can cause a precarious fidelity; and "when the 'forever' is weak – affirms Pope Francis – any reason is valid to leave the path taken."[3] Fidelity and coherence to the cause of Christ are not an instant virtue. They require deep awareness of the human, spiritual, psychological and moral implications of the vocation to consecrated life. *God's* cause transcends, challenges, leads to a decision and a dedication of oneself to and for the service of the Kingdom of God. In this service, personal convictions and community commitments are gifts experienced by the grace of conversion. This grace sustains an authentic fidelity that is far from being sterile. Often it favors the affirmation of oneself, and from a reckless fidelity, which ignores one's own limits, goes beyond one's own possibilities.

2. Fidelity and perseverance were at the center of the intervention of Pope Francis in his address to the Plenary Assembly of the Congregation for Institutes of Consecrated Life and Societies of Apostolic Life on 28 Jan-

---

[3] FRANCIS, *The Strength of a Vocation, A Conversation with Fernando Prado*, USCCB, 2018, Washington, DC, pg. 53.

uary 2017: "We may well say that at this moment faithfulness is being put to the test [...]. We are facing a 'hemorrhage' that is weakening consecrated life and the very life of the Church. The abandonment of consecrated life worries us. It is true that some leave as an act of coherence, because they recognize, after serious discernment, that they never had this vocation. However, others, with the passage of time, are no longer faithful, very often only a few years after professing perpetual vows. What has happened?"[4]

The question raised by Pope Francis cannot fall on deaf ears. In the face of the phenomenon of the abandonment of consecrated and clerical life – a common denominator for diverse situations – the Church has long wondered about the attitude to assume.[5] Consecrated life itself has been repeatedly urged to recognize, discern and accompany uncomfortable situations or crises and not reduce the

---

[4] FRANCIS, *Address* to participants in the Plenary Assembly of the Congregation for Institutes of Consecrated Life and Societies of Apostolic Life, Vatican City, (28 January 2017).

[5] JOHN PAUL II, Post-Synodal Apostolic Exhortation *Pastores dabo vobis*, (15 March 1992), 10.

phenomenon to just an alarming statistical situation without questioning, at the same time, the meaning and implications of fidelity and perseverance to the vocation of the *sequela Christi*. The latter is a journey of conversion and purification. It helps to rediscover the foundation and identity of one's call without giving way to pessimism or to the tiring frustration of those who feel powerless and prepare for the worst.

The complexity and delicacy of these issues in many cases make it difficult to find adequate solutions. It is crucial to possess an attitude of listening and discernment, imploring with trust the light of the Holy Spirit, that we may read the reality in a serious and serene manner. These are situations that, negatively affect the self-understanding of the very identity of consecrated men and women. They cast shadows on the evangelical credibility of the Institutes and undermine, in some way, the trust of the people of God towards the world of consecrated persons.

3. The Congregation for Institutes of Consecrated Life and Societies of Apostolic Life cannot but be challenged by the issues concerning fidelity and perseverance within consecrated life. On the basis of what is most frequently observed in the experience of Institutes and Societies, it has therefore sought to identify some indications or lines of preventive intervention and accompaniment. In this perspective, the present document intends to provide guidelines which, on the basis of the norms of the Code of Canon Law and the practice of the Dicastery, are useful to all consecrated persons, and to all those who have roles of responsibility both in government and in formation.

This document is divided into three parts:

– *Gazing and listening*: monitoring and intercepting situations which can cause uneasiness, discomfort, crisis in the personal and community life of consecrated men and women, without arousing alarm or, on the contrary, endorsing a dangerously underestimated reading of events. In taking on a problem, superiors, brothers and sisters, put themselves in a position to face it. Thus, those who have the honesty and humility to recognize their problems can be helped and accompanied. Problems have faces, stories, biographies; it is a matter of recognizing a brother, a sister in difficulty and, at the same time, recognizing one's own difficulties. "When, in God's presence, we examine our life's journey, no areas can be off limits. In all aspects of life – urges Pope Francis – we can continue to grow and offer something greater to God, even in those areas we find most difficult."[6]

- *Enkindling awareness*: the combination of fidelity-perseverance characterizes the Church's teaching on Consecrated Life. The two terms are perceived as inseparable aspects of a single spiritual attitude. Perseverance is an indispensable quality of fidelity. In this dynamism, we realize the importance of ongoing formation, which demands of both the consecrated person and the Institute "a continual examination regarding fidelity to the Lord; docility to his Spirit; […] constancy in the gift of self; humility in bearing with adversities."[7] In fact, the vocation to consecrated life is a journey of transformation that renews the heart and mind

---

[6] FRANCIS, Apostolic Exhortation *Gaudete et exsultate*, (19 March 2018), 175.

[7] CONGREGATION FOR INSTITUTES OF CONSECRATED LIFE AND SOCIETIES OF APOSTOLIC LIFE, *Potissimum Institutioni*. Directives on Formation in Religious Institutes (2 February 1990), 67.

of the person "*so that they may discern what is the will of God, what is good, pleasing and perfect*" (*Rm* 12:2). "The gift of discernment – says Pope Francis – has become all the more necessary today"[8] to "make us move beyond mere good intentions."[9] As men and women of discernment, consecrated persons become capable of reading the reality of human life in the light of the Spirit, and thus they are able to choose, decide and act according to the divine will.[10] Formation requires a constant exercise of the gift of discernment: "the gift of discernment is what gives the necessary maturity to a consecrated person. This is fundamental in today's consecrated life: adulthood."[11]

---

[8] FRANCIS, Apostolic Exhortation *Gaudete et exsultate*, (19 March 2018), 167.

[9] *Ibid.*, 169.

[10] Cf. CONGREGATION FOR THE CLERGY, *The Gift of the Priestly Vocation, Ratio Fundamentalis Institutionis Sacerdotalis*, (8 December 2016), 43.

[11] FRANCIS, *The Strength of a Vocation, A Conversation with Fernando Prado*, USCCB, 2018, Washington, DC, pg. 42.

— *Separation from the Institute. Norms and practice of the Dicastery*: "In consecrated life one cannot walk alone. We need someone to accompany us."[12] Someone who helps us recognize and correct, attitudes, lifestyles, shortcomings and infidelities that are an evident counter-testimony to the state of consecrated life. Someone who helps us rediscover the sense of discipline since it safeguards a personal orderly type of life, while it promotes care for our brothers and sisters. Discipline shapes the disciple of Christ, not in view of a dull conformism, but towards coherence with one's own form of life in the *sequela Christi*. Discipline teaches the necessary distancing of oneself from worldly mentality and ideologies, which compromise the credibility of our lifestyle. Discipline strengthens the sense of vigilance, an interior attitude of readiness and lucidity when faced with adverse or risky situations. Finally, discipline is an exercise of mercy, because we are debtors of mercy to one another.

---

[12] *Ibid.*, pg. 43.

In the perspective of discernment-accompaniment, superiors and those having responsibilities are offered – at every level – a normative regulatory framework and practices of the Dicastery in order to correctly assess situations of disciplinary importance in full compliance with the procedures established by Canon Law.

4. A journey of fidelity in perseverance demands looking at life as consecrated persons without closing one's eyes when problems or difficulties arise. These can be signs of precarious faithfulness or tendencies towards infidelity. Consecrated persons on a journey of authentic fidelity recognize and discern their own story while, above all, they question themselves about "fidelity born of love."[13] They learn to listen to their own conscience and to cultivate a well-formed conscience gifted with right judgment.[14] They discipline their own life so as not to deprive of meaning the attention to their interior life. They welcome the gift of divine grace, the promise and pledge of *remaining in God's love* (cf. *Jn* 15:9).

---

[13] FRANCIS, Apostolic Exhortation *Gaudete et exsultate*, (19 March 2018), 112.

[14] Cf. CONGREGATION FOR THE CLERGY, *The Gift of the Priestly Vocation, Ratio Fundamentalis Institutionis Sacerdotalis*, (8 December 2016), 94.

Part One
GAZING AND LISTENING

I.
THE PHENOMENON OF DEPARTURES: SOME CRITICAL ISSUES

A phenomenon that questions us

5. The reality of the abandonment of consecrated life is a symptom of a broader crisis, which questions the different forms of life recognized by the Church. This phenomenon cannot be justified solely by referring to socio-cultural causes, nor addressed with a sense of resignation, which leads us to consider it as normal. It is not normal that after a long period of initial formation or after many years in consecrated life one decides to ask to separate from the Institute.

Alongside testimonies of exemplary life, we find, quite often, situations in which we can observe "an intermittent dedication, an occasional fidelity, a selective obedience," and which are perhaps symptoms of "a watered down and mediocre life, devoid of meaning."[1] "Weaknesses and difficulties will emerge to dampen the joy we knew so well at the beginning of our journey."[2] Sometimes persons who have lived with generous dedication and exemplary conduct, exhibit strange behaviors for which it is hard to find the motivations and even harder to accept them. Other times behavioral tendencies explode, occasions of scandal arise, which are hurtful and raise serious questions about the previous formation journey and lifestyle.

However, today as yesterday, "many consecrated people and ministers of God, in silent self-dedication, persevere oblivious to the fact that doing good often makes no noise […]. They continue to believe and to preach courageously the Gospel of grace and mercy to men and women who thirst for reasons to live, to hope and to love. They have no fear before the

---

[1] FRANCIS, *Address* to Bishops participating in the course promoted by the Congregation for Bishops, Vatican City, (13 September 2018).

[2] FRANCIS, *Address on the occasion of the Meeting with the Religious Communities of Korea*, Kkottongnae (Korea), (16 August 2014).

wounds of Christ's flesh, always inflicted by sin and often by the children of the Church."[3]

Forms of discomfort

6. Problematic situations question critical issues and generate the uneasiness or discomfort that are most frequently found in consecrated life in general. Pope Francis acknowledges that these risks and limits also arise from the culture of our time: "We live immersed in the so-called *culture of fragmentation*, of the *provisional.*"[4]

It is a matter of recognizing some of the issues that could be at the origin of different forms of discomfort or more serious and critical problems, before implementing paths of accompaniment, prevention and care. We highlight some that are more relevant and verifiable. From this perspective, it is crucial to recognize

[3] FRANCIS, *Address* to Bishops participating in the course promoted by the Congregation for Bishops, Vatican City, (13 September 2018).

[4] FRANCIS, *Address* to participants in the Plenary Assembly of the Congregation for Institutes of Consecrated Life and Societies of Apostolic Life, Vatican City, (28 January 2017).

the problems and listen to those who are facing them, so as not to be forced later to diagnose situations that tend to be unresolvable.

A watchful gaze and attentive listening

7. We are called to recognize, that is to have a watchful gaze and attentive listening: "the approach of a missionary disciple is an approach nourished by the light and strength of the Holy Spirit;"[5] listening that urges us to be attentive to the other, to pay attention to the brothers and sisters next door. To recognize is "learning to discern and discover" what "keeps us far from real human dramas."[6] It therefore requires humility, closeness and empathy, to perceive and be attuned to "the joys and the hopes, the griefs and the anxieties of the people of this age, especially those who are poor or in any way af-

---

[5] FRANCIS, Apostolic Exhortation *Evangelii gaudium*, (24 November 2013), 50.

[6] FRANCIS, *Homily* on the occasion of the Blessing of the Sacred Pallium for the New Metropolitan Archbishops on the Solemnity of Saints Peter and Paul Apostles, Vatican City, (29 June 2018); cf. FRANCIS, Apostolic Exhortation *Evangelii gaudium*, (24 November 2013), 270.

flicted."[7] The same gaze and the same listening, full of solicitude and care, should be directed toward those who are experiencing conditions of discomfort, uneasiness or crisis. It is a gaze of "compassion […] and not pity. [...] There is no compassion that does not listen and show solidarity with the other." This gaze arises from "the freedom born of love and of the desire to put the good of others before all else."[8]

8. A distracted or shortsighted gaze, that is superficial, is always the cause of misunderstanding, prejudice, suffering and feelings of guilt; it provokes a dangerous confusion between the different levels – psychological, relational and spiritual – of the human experience. The first step in identifying, even strategically, what to do and which steps to take in order to discern and prevent or to accompany through processes of support and care, is to recognize that a brother or a sister is experiencing a peri-

[7] SECOND VATICAN ECUMENICAL COUNCIL, Pastoral Constitution on the Church in the Modern World *Gaudium et spes*, 1.

[8] FRANCIS, *Address* on the occasion of the Meeting with Clergy, Religious and Seminarians, Apostolic Journey to Ecuador, Bolivia and Paraguay (5-13 July 2015), Santa Cruz de la Sierra (Bolivia), (9 July 2015).

od of difficulty. In order to recognize, discern, accompany, it is also necessary to have specific qualifications. This requires a positive and effective interaction of professionals called to initiate paths of spiritual accompaniment, psychotherapy and care.

Crisis of the Institutes: uncertainty and disorientation

9. Throughout its secular history consecrated life has shown an ever-renewed ability to attract[9] those who, searching for meaning, find in it a significant reference model. This attraction needs to be rediscovered and encouraged "in its original attractiveness, as an antidote to the 'paralysis of normality' and as openness to grace that turns the world and its ways of thinking upside-down. Rekindling the allure of evangelical radicalism amongst young generations, so they can rediscover the prophetic value of chastity, poverty and obedience as a harbinger

---

[9] "We can apply to the consecrated life the words of Benedict XVI which I cited in the Apostolic Exhortation *Evangelii Gaudium*: 'It is not by proselytizing that the Church grows, but by attraction.'" FRANCIS, *Apostolic Letter* to All Consecrated People on the occasion of the Year of Consecrated Life, (23 November 2014), II, 1.

of the Kingdom and the complete fulfilment of their lives is something that cannot be neglected at a time dominated by consumeristic and commercialistic mindsets."[10]

Even institutions are going through crises with the risk "of giving more emphasis to the shadows, at the expense of light."[11] Pope Francis notes, with wise realism, that "when, in the life of our communities, we experience a certain 'listlessness,' when we prefer peace and quiet to the newness of God, it is a bad sign. It means that we are trying to find shelter from the wind of the Spirit."[12]

An obscure attraction

10. We are called to rekindle the attractiveness of the radical nature of the Gospel, which is perceived as something obscure, both from

---

[10] XV ORDINARY GENERAL ASSEMBLY OF THE SYNOD OF BISHOPS, *Instrumentum laboris "Young people, the Faith and Vocational Discernment,"* Vatican City 2018, 103.

[11] FRANCIS, *Address* on the occasion of the Meeting with the Clergy, Men and Women Religious, and Permanent Deacons, Pastoral Visit to Pompei and Naples, Naples, (21 March 2015).

[12] FRANCIS, *Homily* on the occasion of the Solemnity of Pentecost, Vatican City, (20 May 2018).

within and outside of us. In fact, discomfort and uneasiness undermine the credibility of this form of life that sees the decline of its appreciation as a global project, being perceived as alien to the culture of our time. Pope Francis has repeatedly emphasized its signs. The Pontiff lists some of them: "individualism, spiritualism, living in a little world, addiction, intransigence, the rejection of new ideas and approaches, dogmatism, nostalgia, pessimism, hiding behind rules and regulations."[13] The consecrated person is not a bureaucrat or a functionary, but a passionate person who cannot live in "dull and dreary mediocrity."[14] In particular, in the *Letter to All Consecrated People* the Pope does not indulge in concessions: "None of us should be dour, discontented and dissatisfied, for 'a gloomy disciple is a disciple of gloom.' Like everyone else, we have our troubles, our dark nights of the soul, our disappointments and infirmities, our experience of slowing down, as we grow older. However, in all these things we should be able to discover 'perfect joy.' For it

---

[13] FRANCIS, Apostolic Exhortation *Gaudete et exsultate*, (19 March 2018), 134.
[14] *Ibid.*, 138.

is here that we learn to recognize the face of Christ, who became like us in all things, and to rejoice in the knowledge that we are being conformed to him who, out of love of us, did not refuse the sufferings of the cross. In a society which exalts the cult of efficiency, fitness and success, one which ignores the poor and dismisses losers, we can witness by our lives to the truth of the words of Scripture: '*When I am weak, then I am strong*' (*2 Cor* 12:10)."[15]

"The temptation of survival turns what the Lord presents as an opportunity for mission into something dangerous, threatening and potentially disastrous. This attitude is not limited to the consecrated life, but we in particular are urged not to fall into it."[16]

The inadequate evaluation of the difficulties

11. We are also invited to overcome a certain reticence in speaking about our difficul-

---

[15] FRANCIS, *Apostolic Letter* to All Consecrated People on the occasion of the Year of Consecrated Life, (23 November 2014), II, 1.

[16] FRANCIS, *Homily* on the occasion of the XXI World Day of Consecrated Life, Vatican City, (2 February 2017).

ties or weaknesses, because in consecrated life every accusation can be turned into a self-accusation: no one can get out of the problems that preoccupy or trouble a community, a province, an Institute. It is not yet evident that uneasiness, discomfort, crisis are opportunities for constructive and calm confrontation and not sterile polemics or, worse, ill-concealed indifference. All this indicates that we are still at the beginning of the journey to overcome a mentality that wants to keep problematic situations almost hidden, for fear or reluctance to expose weaknesses. In contrast, we powerlessly observe the phenomenon – often denounced by Pope Francis – of the "terrorism of gossip" which certainly does not help to create the climate of a serene and respectful community life. When assessing the statistics of one's own Institute, we still find a mentality that interprets these situations as an inevitable result of the disorientation and uncertainty of the times, without wondering if perhaps they are also institutional failures. New admissions are publicized, departures are privatized, with an unconscious tendency to keep a distance from the latter.

II.
INSTANCES TO BE INTERPRETED AND DYNAMICS TO BE CONVERTED

Identity building processes

12. Weaknesses, difficulties, fragility – at the origin of the discomfort – can be traced back to identity building processes which, in the current cultural context, have become increasingly complex both at the level of awareness/consciousness and at the level of identification/differentiation, and therefore of acceptance of oneself and of one's own incompleteness. The difficulty for self-identification both in the psychosexual component and in the cognitive and emotional dimension is at the origin of many forms of relational discomfort and maladjustment and even serious forms of psychopathology. The *crisis* lexicon and its declinations seem to be the common denominator of very different situations, often including extreme existential tendencies. Whether the crisis occurs or is resolved as a risk or an opportunity, this can only be verified by its results. Disorders which wound the humanity of the consecrated person can become an opportunity for purification, transformation and wisdom through the necessary experience of grace which renders possible obedience to the call (cf. *2 Cor* 12:9).

In the perspective of the paschal mystery, the admission of one's own fragility or weakness shows that the limits related to our condition as mortal beings, invite us to consider the environment around us with eyes of trust and not with suspicion, as if someone wanted to surprise us in our presumed or real shortcomings. Narrow-mindedness fuels mistrust and does not reduce possible risks and damage, or the fear of failure. In any case, trust in the faithfulness of God who supports us and on whom we can count is diminished. Trust is the principle of every salvific action. The call to follow God's Son entails surrendering oneself to this trust, even in the experience of infidelity and sin. God, by giving Christ to human history, has made him the *source of eternal life for all those who obey Him* (*Heb* 5:9).

Faith: an illusory light

13. "Trust must grow – says Pope Francis – precisely when circumstances throw us to the ground."[17] These circumstances are sometimes marked by the suffering caused by bitter trials endured inside or outside the Institute; failures, often involuntary and at times voluntary, where trust in God is excluded and a lack of self-confidence prevails. Then other idols take over which "cause a great existential emptiness."[18] In this emptiness, faith appears as "an illusory light"[19] and ends up "being associated with darkness [...]. In the absence of light everything becomes confused; it is impossible to discern good from evil or the road to our destination from other roads which take us in endless cir-

---

[17] Francis, *Homily* on the occasion of the Celebration of Vespers and Te Deum on the occasion of the Bicentennial of the Re-establishment of the Society of Jesus, Rome, (27 September 2014).

[18] Francis, *Address* to participants in the Plenary Assembly of the Congregation for Institutes of Consecrated Life and Societies of Apostolic Life, Vatican City, (28 January 2017).

[19] Francis, Encyclical Letter *Lumen fidei*, (29 June 2013), 2.

cles, going nowhere."[20] It is not a journey into the night, but the collapse of the journey, up to the decision, sometimes sudden and without dialogue and encounter, to leave the Institute. This decision sometimes conceals the refusal to be helped, denying the possibility of being visited again *from on high* (*Lk* 1:78).

No less worrisome is the condition of those who survive the absence of God, while remaining in community life. Consciously or not, an atmosphere of discomfort spreads, which at times makes brothers, sisters and superiors, incapable of finding solutions to stem the tension and uneasiness that risks compromising the stability of the community.

The way of understanding and living consecrated celibacy

14. When there is a difficulty in constructing one's identity, it affects the way consecrated celibacy is understood and lived. The so-called affective crises are subject to many variables and difficult situations, not without dramatic implications. A narcissistic cultural context

[20] *Ibid.*, 3.

that tends to enhance pleasure and claims freedom without limits, especially in the sphere of emotional and sexual life, cannot be said to be irrelevant. Rarely do the words of the Pontiff resonate so severely: "one of the worst attitudes of a religious: to mirror himself, narcissism."[21] The identity crisis makes it more difficult to understand and live consecrated celibacy as an identity and as a project. The processes required in this journey towards maturity presuppose a lucid and available decision-making capacity and a love free from the need for possession, against all forms of affective dependence. Furthermore, naive attitudes in the way of experiencing friendship and interpersonal relationships should not be underestimated. A greater realism and a better understanding of one's limits should lead to greater prudence. If we are aware of our weakness, we are not under the illusion of being able to control our feelings and the passions they generate.

[21] FRANCIS, *Address* on the occasion of the Audience to Young Consecrated Persons, Vatican City, (17 September 2015).

A liquid fidelity

15. The difficulty in understanding consecrated celibacy cannot disregard the so-called "bonding issue." This problem must be taken into serious consideration, both to understand and to prevent some phenomena that inevitably lead to the loss of perseverance, and to help, accompany and treat those who manifest forms of relational and psychic discomfort or various forms of maladjustment. The world of consecrated men and women is exposed to a pervasive culture of dissipation or consumption of feelings: remaining faithful is no longer taken for granted, and even less so is remaining faithful for life. Fidelity is an integral part of freedom and allows the person who is searching-discerning to be formed in the light of truth and goodness properly understood. The current crisis of fidelity goes hand in hand with the crisis of identity and is linked to the crisis of the sense of belonging to institutions, as it is believed that every bond impoverishes or hinders freedom. The gift of self in following the Lord is the gift of one's life out of love; but today it seems that even this gift can have a time limit. In fact, the fragility of bonds is not exposed in order to find a remedy to it but is often indicated as an evolutionary sign of our civilization.

The meaning of a rule-oriented bond

16. To the critical issues already mentioned, we must add the influence of a misunderstood concept of freedom, which relativizes the sense of a rule-oriented bond. This mentality is reinforced by a widespread language that tends to devalue the sense of mediation of institutions and rules. This can fuel a misleading sense of autonomy invoked in the name of spontaneity, impulsiveness, and the claiming of one's own space even when these can compromise the search for the common good. Mediations offer opportunities – for everyone – to enhance the human, spiritual, professional and last but not least, they are also normative resources. No one hides their limits, which upon inspection, are also our limits. The mediations of institutions and rules in consecrated life encourage us to consider ourselves as brothers and sisters in the bond of fraternity. Individualism and so-called parallel paths often open the way to departure. To the extent that emphasis is placed on individuality, one turns away from the commitment to consider that one's own well-being is linked to and dependent on that of the community and therefore the need to increase the coherence of all in fidelity to following a Rule.

Relationship with time and space

17. Another key point to correctly interpret this discomfort is the relationship with time and space, essential elements of all growth and development. Transitions and age-related challenges and/or crises highlight the importance of a correct relationship with time and space. In particular, wasting time impoverishes fidelity and perseverance. We run the risk of living an alienated, worldly time; a time of "everything right away," a day-to-day life; with a superficiality that results in instability, not only of temperament, but above all in ministry, with recurring requests for transfers. Such a phenomenon is far from marginal in our environments. Knowing how to manage time is a sign of a healthy autonomy and, therefore, of a mature ability to choose. The phenomenon of consecrated persons on the verge of *burnout* and of those, on the other hand, who are practically jobless, must not be underestimated. Both phenomena can be found in consecrated life. Consecrated persons have made a covenant with God and with their brothers and sisters. Therefore, the time in which they live is within the covenant with the *faithful witness,* Jesus Christ (cf. *Rev* 3:14), the One who will also ask for an account of their time.

Difficult interpersonal and community relationships

18. The situation of uneasiness created by the difficulty – and sometimes impossibility – of relationships and interpersonal communication is another critical issue, at the origin of multiple forms of discomfort or fragility. In consecrated life, fraternity suffers setbacks to the point of justifying mediocre lifestyles, occasional gatherings, and a toleration for living together. When interpersonal relationships are reduced to formal reciprocal respect, to mere encounters in view of service, to common acts punctuated by the clock; when community meetings are lived as obligations and variations to the daily routine are seen as threats to the quiet life, conditions are set for the progressive emptying of the sense of fraternity. It should come as no surprise that the first departure is achieved by distancing oneself from one's own community. Against these temptations Pope Francis urges us to reclaim the value of community life which preserves us from the "growing consumerist individualism that tends to isolate us in a quest for wellbeing apart from others."[22]

The experience of solitude

19. Difficulties related to interpersonal relationships can trigger, especially in consecrated life, the discomfort of a widespread and painful experience of solitude – as a personal experience – even in contexts where the attention and involvement of brothers and sisters is vibrant. The solitude of a consecrated person can expose risks. Being surrounded by brothers and sisters – people with whom one lives with or with whom one is bound by ties of esteem and friendship – is an opportunity that helps to break the circle of isolation in which one encloses oneself. Solitude turns into isolation when it leads to "finding refuge in our own certainties and comfort zones, of indifference to others and division into 'cliques.' […] These are situations which lead to a kind of isolation and dissatisfaction, a sadness that slowly gives rise

[22] Francis, Apostolic Exhortation *Gaudete et exsultate*, (19 March 2018), 146.

to resentment, to constant complaint, to boredom."[23] Solitude, on the other hand, becomes fruitful when it is inhabited by the presence of God to whom we surrender our life, and by the presence of brothers and sisters, a providential presence, which helps us come out of ourselves to rediscover the gift of the other.

Tension between community and mission

20. Another critical element can be seen in the tension between community and mission, positively understood as a "tension in the fundamental sense, the tension of fidelity."[24] This tension, if not overcome or resolved, can lead to conflicts; dissatisfaction and/or disappointment, especially when associated with activism or individualism. It can be an opportunity for creativity and innovation if it is seen as an opportunity for investing new energies and for

[23] FRANCIS, *Homily*, Apostolic Journey to Cuba, to the United States of America and Visit to the United Nations Headquarters (19-28 September 2015), La Habana (Cuba), (20 September 2015).

[24] FRANCIS, *Address* on the occasion of the Meeting with the Consecrated Men and Women of the Diocese of Rome, Vatican City, (16 May 2016).

joint projects. A fruitful elaboration of this tension leads to a personal and community change which "consists in a conversion of our own gaze: trying to see each other in God, and also being able to see ourselves from the other's point of view: namely, it presents a two-fold challenge linked to the quest for unity [...] within the religious communities. ..."[25] One can well understand that unresolved tensions, often degenerating into open conflict, fuel dissatisfaction with the community, undermine the sense of belonging to the Institute and ultimately, can discourage one's life choice to such an extent that abandoning the Institute is considered the only way out.

Management of the digital world

21. In our communities, particularly in problematic community situations, an ineffective use of the digital world can occur and, consequently, the search for refuge in the commu-

---

[25] FRANCIS, *Address* to participants in the Ecumenical Colloquium of Men and Women Religious held by the Congregation for Institutes of Consecrated Life and Societies of Apostolic Life, Vatican City, (24 January 2015).

nication spaces offered by new technologies, especially by *social media*. As Pope Francis reminds us: "This is not to say that certain problems do not exist. The speed with which information is communicated exceeds our capacity for reflection and judgement, and this does not make for more balanced and proper forms of self-expression. The variety of opinions being aired can be seen as helpful, but it also enables people to barricade themselves behind sources of information, which only confirm their own wishes and ideas, or political and economic interests. The world of communications can help us either to expand our knowledge or to lose our bearings. The desire for digital connectivity can have the effect of isolating us from our neighbors, from those closest to us."[26] Furthermore, we cannot avoid questioning the type of bonds that are established through media communication, which is increasingly widespread and frequent in our communities. Forms of psychological dependence are growing which open the way to other forms of discomfort

[26] FRANCIS, *Message* for the 48th World Communication Day, *Communication at the Service of an Authentic Culture of Encounter*, (1 June 2014).

and fragility: "Digital media – Pope Francis observes – can expose people to the risk of addiction, isolation and gradual loss of contact with concrete reality, blocking the development of authentic interpersonal relationships. New forms of violence are spreading through *social media*, such as *cyberbullying*. The *internet* is also a channel for spreading pornography and the exploitation of persons for sexual purposes or through gambling."[27]

Relationship with power and possession

22. While present in every human relationship, "the thirst for power and worldly interests often stands in our way."[28] "It is striking that even some who clearly have solid doctrinal and spiritual convictions frequently fall into a lifestyle which leads to an attachment to financial security or to a desire for power or human glory at all cost, rather than giving their lives to

---

[27] FRANCIS, Post-Synodal Apostolic Exhortation *Christus vivit*, (25 March 2019), 88.

[28] FRANCIS, Apostolic Exhortation *Gaudete et exsultate*, (19 March 2018), 91.

others in mission."[29] The document *New Wine in New Wineskins* expressed concern about the "permanence of government styles and practices that move away from or contradict the spirit of service, to the point of degenerating into forms of authoritarianism."[30]

---

[29] FRANCIS, Apostolic Exhortation *Evangelii gaudium*, (24 November 2013), 80.

[30] CONGREGATION FOR INSTITUTES OF CONSECRATED LIFE AND SOCIETIES OF APOSTOLIC LIFE, *Guidelines. New Wine in New Wineskins. The Consecrated Life and its Ongoing Challenges since Vatican II*, Rome (6 January 2017), 43.

Part Two

ENKINDLING AWARENESS

I.
FIDELITY AND PERSEVERANCE

Memoria Dei

23. Fidelity is measured by time, history and everyday life. If fidelity is an essential virtue of every interpersonal relationship, perseverance is the specific virtue of time: both of them question the relationship with the other. In the present time, fragmented and without constraints, these realities are a challenge for each person and, in particular for Christians. But how can we recognize our own fidelity if not by drawing from the fidelity of the One who is faithful (cf. *1 Thess* 5:24) and from faith in Him? The faithful one is the one who holds together the memory and the present: this enables him to persevere. Indeed, perseverance cannot but be sustained by the *memoria Dei*. In this sense the Christian, capable of the *memoria Dei*, knows and remembers the Lord's action.

It is a memory that engages the heart of the person, the seat of one's will and mind. An ever-renewed memory of the divine fidelity is what generates and sustains the fidelity of the believer.

God is the Faithful One

24. Pope Francis often urges us to remember Christ's love of predilection, and states: "We can say something about the spousal love of Jesus for the Church," a love that has "three features: it is faithful, it perseveres – he never tires of loving his Church, and it is fruitful. [...] Fidelity is the very being of Jesus' love."[1]

The themes of *fidelity* and *perseverance* are central to the Word of God. Fidelity, *hesed*, is, in fact, one of the principal attributes of God: God is the Faithful One. The whole history of salvation is nothing other than the story of this covenant between God and creation, between God and his people, Israel, between God and all humanity. Goodness and fidelity characterize

---

[1] FRANCIS, *Daily Meditation* in the Chapel of *Domus Sanctae Marthae*, (2 June 2014), in: *L'Osservatore Romano*, Italian daily edition, year CLIV, n. 124, Tues. 03/06/2014.

the nature of God and all His actions towards the chosen people, but also towards creation.

God promises to never betray his covenant, but to remain faithful forever. God overcomes indignation and takes on the evil of humanity, so that humanity can be faithful to him once again in the freedom regained through forgiveness. This constant loyalty to the covenant is nothing other than God's fidelity to his promise. The prophet Hosea speaks of God's fidelity as a fruit of God's tenacious love for his people through the suggestive image of marriage: "*Therefore, behold, I will draw her to me, I will lead her into the desert, and I will speak to her heart [...]. In that day I will make a covenant for them [...] I will make you my bride forever, I will make you my bride in justice and in uprightness, in benevolence and in love, I will betroth you to myself in fidelity and you will know the Lord*" (*Hos* 2:16ff.). The evident and continued fragility of Israel, both as a people and as individuals, does not weaken the *rock* (*Dt* 32:4) of God's faithfulness, as the psalmist sings: *Your faithfulness from generation to generation* (*Ps* 119:90).

Christ, iconic image of fidelity

25. From this comes the human response: a fidelity that is above all *faith and trust* (as expressed in the Greek translation of fidelity, which uses the terms *pistis/pisteuein* [faith/to believe] and its derivatives), reliance upon and adherence to the promises and precepts of the covenant. *All the paths of the Lord are steadfast love and faithfulness, for those who keep his covenant and his decrees* (*Ps* 25:10).

Even though Israel was not a *faithful servant*, has gone astray and has repeated the infidelity of the generation who crossed the desert – *a stubborn and rebellious generation whose hearts were not loyal to God and whose spirits were not faithful to God* (*Ps* 78:8) – God has not ceased to demonstrate his fidelity: *he has compassion on us with everlasting love* (*Is* 54:8).

The theme of the relationship and the renewal of the relationship, in spite of the infidelity and of the evil of humanity, characterizes the whole history of salvation until the coming of Jesus. He is his Father's faithful one and, therefore, the faithful one to the weak humanity, prone to evil, to whom he constantly offers his promise of salvation. Jesus Christ is the 'Amen' of fidelity (cf. *2 Cor* 1:20; *Rev* 3:14). The coming of Christ, his Incarnation, is the fulfilment of the promise. Jesus is the *faithful witness*, as expressed in the Book of Revelation

(1:5), the *trustworthy and true servant* (*Rev* 19:11) in whom all things *written in the Law of Moses, in the Prophets and in the Psalms were destined to be fulfilled* (*Lk* 24:44). In him all God's promises are fulfilled (cf. *2 Cor* 1:20). God's fidelity is manifested in Christ (cf. *1 Thess* 5:23-24).

Christ, the faithful witness, teaches fidelity to humanity, he is an image of fidelity; he is faithful to God the Father. He invites every person to be faithful to his Word. Grace is given to us and we are invited to respond with *fidelity* to the Father through the Son who loved us and gave himself for us. One of the first titles given to Christians was that of *believers*, to indicate their faith in Christ (*Acts* 10:45; *Eph* 1:1*)*, animated by love (*Jn* 15:9f). Paul makes frequent use of this word, both for people and attitudes, and mentions *fidelity* among the fruits of the Spirit (*Gal* 5:22).

"We can never achieve this faithfulness by our own efforts; it is not only the fruit of our daily striving; it comes from God and is founded on the 'yes' of Christ who said: my food is to do the will of the Father (cf. *Jn* 4:34). It is into this 'yes' that we must enter, into this 'yes' of Christ, into adherence to God's will, in order to reach the point of saying with St. Paul that it is not we who live but Christ himself who lives in us."[2]

Fidelity is nourished by encounters

26. The encounter with God touches the totality of the person. In this encounter we are called to live the total surrender of ourselves: intellect and will, mind and heart, with the firmness and sweetness of our consent. Faith is the mystery of the encounter generated by the Spirit, between the Father and the Son in the heart of every person who welcomes the Word and accepts to be conformed to Him.

Encountering the Lord opens the disciple to the fullness of life. This participation in the life of the Trinity manifests itself in a style in which God is everything and everything refers to Him: *For you have indeed stripped yourself of the old person with his actions and have put on the new self, which is being renewed, in knowledge, in the image of his Creator* (*Col* 3:9). The Trinity lives in the life of those who respond to the call *to follow Christ* with the gift of their whole self: "The consecrated life proclaims what the Father, through

---

[2] BENEDICT XVI, *General Audience*, Vatican City, (30 May 2012).

the Son and in the Spirit, brings about by his love, his goodness and his beauty."[3]

To persevere: memory and hope

27. The term *perseverance* appears in the Synoptic Gospels with an identical expression in Matthew and Mark: *Anyone who perseveres to the end will be saved* (*Mt* 10:22b; 24:13; *Mk* 13:13); and has a similar content in Luke: *Your perseverance will win you your life* (*Lk* 21:19).

Jesus himself, in the solemn context of the Easter supper, directly and personally invites his disciples to persevere: *You are the ones who persevered with me in my trials* (*Lk* 22:28). He announces to his disciples that they will have to endure his same trials; and he seems to recognize his own by their willingness to endure his trials for as long as he persevered, to the point of giving his life for them (cf. *Jn* 13:1). Jesus urges his disciples – not only to persevere to the end – but to persevere in the custody of the Word heard *with a noble and generous heart* (*Lk* 8:15) and in bearing fruit. Scripture is also a source of perseverance, of consolation and

---

[3] JOHN PAUL II, Post-Synodal Apostolic Exhortation *Vita consecrata*, (25 March 1996), 20.

hope, and at the same time, the cause of persecutions to be faced (cf. *Rm* 15:4).

The Gospel texts already present some of the characteristic themes of the subsequent New Testament discussion on *perseverance*, as a necessary and qualifying characteristic of Christians. The Letter of James opens, in an exemplary manner, precisely with an exhortation to perseverance: *Consider it all joy, my brothers and sisters, when you encounter various trials, for you know that the testing of your faith produces perseverance. And let perseverance be perfect, so that you may be perfect and complete, lacking in nothing* (*Jas* 1:2-4).

Perseverance is understood first of all as *patience*, as the ability to undergo trials that prepare us to be *perfect and complete*.

Perseverance, as lived and witnessed by Paul, is the virtue of those who fight to bear witness of fidelity to Christ (*1 Tm* 6:11-12). Christians are called to perseverance after the example of Christ, as Jesus himself affirmed (cf. *Lk* 22:28).

28. The Letter to the Hebrews calls us to *persevere in running the race that lies before us while keeping our eyes fixed on Jesus, the leader and perfecter of faith* (*Heb* 12:1-2). In perseverance authentic love for Christ is revealed, a love that fixes the eyes of the heart and mind on Him, as an athlete does when fixing his eyes on the finish line. When life has no purpose, everything becomes heavy, devoid of meaning and love shows its instability.

"The author of the letter to the Hebrews says: 'Indeed you only need perseverance, so that you may do the will of God and receive what is promised.' Perseverance to reach the promise. And the path of promise, has beautiful moments, bright moments, and dark moments."[4] The Pope recommends that we always persevere, following the two indications proposed by the Apostle: memory and hope. Remember "the happy days of the encounter with the Lord for example," or "when we have done a good deed and felt Jesus' presence nearby […] or when we chose to enter the seminary, the consecrated life."[5] The author of the letter suggests recalling 'those early days when everything was luminous.' The second indication is 'hope:' "when the devil attacks us with temptations, with vices, with our wretchedness, we should always look to the Lord, the endur-

---

[4] FRANCIS, *Daily Meditation* in the Chapel of *Domus Sanctae Marthae*, *Memory and Hope*, (1 February 2019).

[5] *Ibid.*

ance of the cross, remembering the first beautiful moments of love, of the encounter with the Lord and the hope we are charged with."[6]

The perseverance of consecrated persons is also a gift of the God of the covenant: "the unspoken but eloquent witness of religious to the faithful God whose love is without end."[7] Consecrated life, born of the living experience of the Love that saves, in the light of the fidelity of God the Father, Son and Holy Spirit, finds its meaning in the dynamism of fidelity.[8]

To persevere in fidelity

29. Starting from the Conciliar documents, the combination "fidelity-perseverance" has characterized the magisterial teaching on consecrated life. The Council, as well as post-conciliar documents, do not consider the two terms as synonyms but as inseparable aspects of a single

---

[6] *Ibid.*

[7] CONGREGATION FOR RELIGIOUS AND SECULAR INSTITUTES, *Essential Elements in the Church's Teaching on Religious Life as Applied to Institutes Dedicated to Works of the Apostolate*, Rome, (31 May 1983), 37.

[8] Cf. JOHN PAUL II, Post-Synodal Apostolic Exhortation *Vita consecrata*, (25 March 1996), 70.

spiritual attitude: perseverance is an essential attribute of fidelity. In the documents of the Council and in those immediately following, perseverance appears in a particular way as a typical attribute of fidelity, one of its constitutive qualities, which is combined with humility.

Number 46 of the Dogmatic Constitution *Lumen gentium*, explicitly expresses the greatness of the life of special consecration which prolongs the presence of Christ in history, through the sign and the work of consecrated persons: "this Sacred Synod encourages and praises the men and women, Brothers and Sisters, who in monasteries, or in schools and hospitals, or in the missions, adorn the Bride of Christ by their unswerving and humble faithfulness in their chosen consecration and render generous services of all kinds to mankind."[9] The very life of consecrated men and women is therefore defined by their persevering and humble fidelity to consecration.

Total and exclusive love

30. St. Paul VI, in his teaching on the priesthood and on consecrated life, underlines the

---

[9] Second Vatican Ecumenical Council, Dogmatic Constitution on the Church *Lumen gentium*, 46.

significance of a persevering fidelity, and of the total gift of self of consecrated persons. The Holy Father, even when he does not mention it directly, describes perseverance as an assurance that consecrated persons have irrevocably offered their lives and are fully faithful to their offering.

In the Encyclical Letter *Sacerdotalis caelibatus* of 1967, on the celibacy of priests, he exhorts to authentic love which is "genuine, is all-embracing, stable and lasting, an irresistible spur to all forms of heroism."[10] In the same year, in his *Message for World Vocations Day*, he again emphasizes the totality of the call to a life of special consecration: "The word vocation acquires fullness of meaning, which certainly tends to become, if not exclusive, specific and perfect, where there is a two-fold special vocation: because it comes directly from God like a ray of dazzling light in the most intimate and profound recesses of consciousness; and because it practically expresses itself in the total oblation of life to the one and only supreme love: love of God and love of brothers and sis-

---

[10] PAUL VI, Encyclical Letter *Sacerdotalis caelibatus*, (24 June 1967), 24.

ters, the latter deriving from the first and is one thing with it."[11]

Particularly insightful is the Apostolic Exhortation *Evangelica testificatio* of 1971, in which St. Paul VI asks men and women religious to be witnesses, for the men and women of their time, of a life of unity and openness, which can only be achieved through personal adherence to the Living God.[12] The Pope links the witness of consecrated persons with the perseverance of their lives.

The theme of fidelity acquires particular emphasis in the teaching of St. Paul VI. He calls Secular Institutes, to the "duty to be faithful," faithful "to their own vocation," which must express itself first of all in fidelity to prayer "the foundation of strength and fruitfulness."[13]

In subsequent documents fidelity is increasingly described as a dynamic of growth, in which perseverance requires the necessary

[11] PAUL VI, *Message for the IV World Day of Prayer for Vocations*, (5 March 1967).

[12] Cf. PAUL VI, Apostolic Exhortation *Evangelica testificatio*, (29 June 1971), 34.

[13] PAUL VI, *Address* to the Executive Councils of the Secular Institutes of four Continents, Vatican City, (25 August 1976).

and consistent commitment of consecrated persons, and of Institutes themselves. Perseverance takes on ever more clearly the value of witnessing to God's fidelity to the covenant established with the consecrated person, even before being established by the consecrated person himself or herself.

During the Synod on Consecrated Life the relationship between fidelity and perseverance was increasingly deepened, and fidelity was considered as a key term to summarize and describe the various essential values of consecrated life.

Mary model of perseverance

31. The Virgin Mary is constantly referred to as the model and support of this 'perseverance in fidelity' of consecrated persons. St. John Paul II in the conclusion of the Exhortation *Redemptionis donum* invokes her: "Among all persons consecrated unreservedly to God, she is the first. She – the Virgin of Nazareth – is also the *one most fully consecrated to God*, consecrated in the most perfect way. [...] Persevering in fidelity to Him who is faithful, strive to find a very special *support in Mary!* For she was called by God to the most perfect communion with His

Son. May she, the faithful Virgin, also be the Mother of your evangelical way: may she help you to experience and to show to the world *how infinitely faithful is God Himself!*"[14]

The expression 'perseverance in fidelity' constitutes one of the most effective interpretative keys for reading the Apostolic Exhortation *Vita consecrata*. In it, perseverance is in direct relation with fidelity itself, beyond its various expressions. Perseverance, even before being associated with fidelity to the rule or the charism, is related precisely to fidelity to God, as a sort of synthesis of the whole path of reflection of the Magisterium.

A path of increasing fidelity

32. Throughout salvation history God's fidelity towards every man and woman manifests itself in creativity. Therefore, our fidelity is the opposite of immobility, it is called to be dynamic, as *Vita consecrata*[15] emphasizes: what we want to preserve must be continually updated.

---

[14] JOHN PAUL II, Apostolic Exhortation *Redemptionis donum*, (24 March 1984), 17.

[15] Cf. JOHN PAUL II, Post-Synodal Apostolic Exhortation *Vita consecrata*, (25 March 1996), 70.

Faithfulness is therefore combined with creativity: something must change, and something must be retained. It is important to discern what must be retained in perseverance from what we can and must change.

"This is the meaning of the call to consecrated life: it is an initiative coming wholly from the Father (cf. *Jn* 15:16), who asks those whom he has chosen to respond with complete and exclusive devotion. The experience of this gracious love of God is so deep and so powerful that the person called senses the need to respond by unconditionally dedicating his or her life to God, consecrating to him all things present and future, and placing them in his hands."[16]

If absolute fidelity to the special communion of love with the Father means fidelity to the vocation, to the consecration and to the mission received by the Father, fidelity to Christ is founded not only on baptism but on the spousal covenant. "We may say – writes St. John Paul II *in Vita consecrata* – that the spiritual life, understood as life in Christ or life according to

---

[16] JOHN PAUL II, Post-Synodal Apostolic Exhortation *Vita consecrata*, (25 March 1996), 17.

the Spirit, presents itself as a path of increasing faithfulness, on which the consecrated person is guided by the Spirit and configured by him to Christ, in full communion of love and service in the Church." [17] Being conformed to Christ comes before every service, every action, so that the fidelity to Christ of consecrated men and women enables them to be the extension in history of the special presence of the Risen One. [18]

It is precisely in fidelity to the Holy Spirit[19] that every consecrated person can be ever more faithful to his or her own identity,[20] to the extent that virginity for the Kingdom "is a reflection of the *infinite love* which links the three Divine Persons in the mysterious depths of the life of the Trinity. It is a love to which the Incarnate Word bears witness even to the point of giving his life. It is a love '*poured into our hearts through the Holy Spirit*' (*Rm* 5:5), which evokes a response of total love for God and the brethren."[21]

[17] *Ibid.*, (25 March 1996), 93.
[18] Cf. *Ibid.*, 19.
[19] Cf. *Ibid.*, 62.
[20] Cf. *Ibid.*, 71.
[21] *Ibid.*, 21.

33. In this Trinitarian light we understand the four classic fidelities: "Be always ready, faithful to Christ, the Church, to your Institute and to the men and women of our time."[22] Fidelity to the Institute refers explicitly to the Trinity to the extent that each charism is a gift of God who considers human persons as collaborators: in this sense, personal fidelity to remain in a particular Institute, while admitting exceptions, is not only a human question but it refers to the most profound choice of fidelity to God. Fidelity to the people of our time means to love and serve them according to the heart of Christ and modelled on the Trinity. A fidelity founded on the Trinitarian model is, in essence, like that of God for humanity, it is total fidelity to the extent that it goes all the way to the cross.[23]

Perseverance on the path of holiness

34. Consecrated persons, therefore, are called by vocation to live discipleship and the following of Christ. It is a response of love which implies total adherence to Christ in the

---
[22] *Ibid.*, 110.
[23] Cf. *Ibid.*, 86.

gift of all of one's life, if necessary up to the offering of oneself in martyrdom.

St. John Paul II reaffirmed that an authentic perseverance in the following of Christ, including the aspect of martyrdom, must be lived by consecrated men and women in the simple and ordinary practice of a constant relationship to their foundational charism.[24]

The perseverance of consecrated persons consists in following the path provided by the rules and constitutions of their Institutes, which coincides with the path of holiness in which they are called to persevere, in order to be conformed to Christ, so that they can be witnesses and collaborators in Christ's redemptive work.

For communities as well as for individual consecrated persons, the *sequela Christi* is fulfilled in the paschal mystery, to be lived in that "unwavering trust in the Lord of history"[25] which finds its realization and its most evident testimony precisely in perseverance.

On the other hand, *Vita consecrata* recalls how "in this century, as in other periods of his-

[24] Cf. *Ibid.*, 37.
[25] *Ibid.*, 63

tory, consecrated men and women have borne witness to Christ the Lord with the gift of their own lives. Thousands of them have been forced into the catacombs by the persecution of totalitarian regimes or of violent groups, or have been harassed while engaged in missionary activity, in action on behalf of the poor, in assisting the sick and marginalized; yet they lived and continue to live their consecration in prolonged and heroic suffering, and often with the shedding of their blood, being perfectly configured to the Crucified Lord."[26] To these women and men, who persevered in love to the point of giving their lives, the apostolic exhortation entrusts the duty of interceding for the fidelity of all consecrated persons.[27]

Fraternal life: a place of perseverance

35. After the Council, the Magisterium developed and deepened a constant reflection on the role of fraternal life in the perseverance of consecrated persons. In fact, with growing determination, fraternal life in community and the relationships established within it, have

[26] *Ibid.*, 86.
[27] *Ibid.*

been recognized as one of the characteristic aspects of the *sequela Christi* of consecrated persons. On the other hand, it is very significant that in Conciliar teaching, common life is precisely identified as the first subject of the call to perseverance: "Common life, fashioned on the model of the early Church where the body of believers was united in heart and soul (cf. *Acts* 4:32), and given new force by the teaching of the Gospel, the sacred liturgy and especially the Eucharist, should continue to be lived in prayer and the communion of the same spirit."[28] The apostolic community of Jerusalem, therefore, is proposed as a model of religious life, so that it can meet the challenges of contemporary history.

The Magisterium recommends the means by which fraternal life is renewed and nourished: the Gospel, the Eucharistic Liturgy and prayer. These means will be constantly suggested in subsequent documents, and they will find further development in the Instruction *Starting*

---

[28] Cf. SECOND VATICAN ECUMENICAL COUNCIL, Decree on the adaptation and renewal of Religious Life *Perfectae caritatis*, (28 October 1965), 15.

afresh from Christ.[29] It is gradually pointed out that for a true life of communion not only is prayer essential, but so is the perseverance of the individual members of the community in their personal journey of adhesion to Christ, which is also realized through the care of community relationships. It is also noted that the perseverance of each one is in a reciprocal relationship with the perseverance of the community.

Co-responsible for the fidelity of brothers and sisters

36. The strong connection between an authentically evangelical fraternal life and the effective capacity of a community to form young religious has been amply reaffirmed and deepened by the Directives *Potissimum institutioni*.[30] By making reference, once again, to the "fundamental inspiration" of the Church, described

---

[29] CONGREGATION FOR INSTITUTES OF CONSECRATED LIFE AND SOCIETIES OF APOSTOLIC LIFE, Instruction *Starting Afresh from Christ. A Renewed Commitment to Consecrated Life in the Third Millennium*, (19 May 2002).

[30] CONGREGATION FOR INSTITUTES OF CONSECRATED LIFE AND SOCIETIES OF APOSTOLIC LIFE, *Potissimum institutioni*. Directives on Formation in Religious Institutes, (2 February 1990).

in the Acts of the Apostles, as "the fruit of the Lord's Passover," the document recalls the conditions and the demands that such a model requires:[31] humble realism and an attitude of faith, self-denial and welcoming the gift of the Spirit, all characteristics proper to perseverance.

37. The Instruction *Fraternal Life in Community, Congregavit nos in unum Christi amor*[32] marks the full maturation of the fundamental value of common life, as a support and pledge for perseverance. "The quality of fraternal life – the Instruction affirms – has a significant impact on the perseverance of individual religious. Just as the poor quality of fraternal life has frequently been mentioned by many as the reason for leaving religious life, fraternity lived fully has often been, and still is, a valuable support for the perseverance of many. Within a truly fraternal community, each member has a sense of co-responsibility for the faithfulness of the other; each one contributes to a serene climate

---

[31] Cf. *Ibid.*, 26.

[32] CONGREGATION FOR INSTITUTES OF CONSECRATED LIFE AND SOCIETIES OF APOSTOLIC LIFE, Instruction *Fraternal Life in Community. Congregavit nos in unum Christi amor*, (2 February 1994).

of sharing life, understanding, mutual help; each is attentive to moments of fatigue, suffering, isolation or lack of motivation in others; each offers support to those who are saddened by difficulties and trials. Thus, religious communities, in the support they give to the perseverance of their members, also acquire the value of a sign of the abiding fidelity of God, and thus become a support to the faith and fidelity of Christians who are immersed in the events of this world, where the paths of fidelity seem to be less and less known."[33]

38. The community aspects of perseverance can be found in the most recent documents, with additional significant focus. The Instruction *Starting Afresh from Christ* properly identifies formation as the privileged place for the persevering commitment of both the Institute and the consecrated person.[34] Finally, the Instruction, *The Service of Authority and Obedi-*

[33] *Ibid.*, 57.

[34] Cf. CONGREGATION FOR INSTITUTES OF CONSECRATED LIFE AND SOCIETIES OF APOSTOLIC LIFE, Instruction *Starting Afresh from Christ. A Renewed Commitment to Consecrated Life in the Third Millennium*, (19 May 2002), 18.

ence,[35] entrusts to the superiors, as guarantors and promoters of fraternal life authentically lived according to the Gospel, the care and interest for the perseverance of each religious entrusted to them.[36]

Persevering in prayer

39. In the Magisterial documents the theme of prayer characterizes the relationship between perseverance and fidelity. The first support for perseverance that consecrated persons are invited to give attention to lies in continuous prayer for the grace of fidelity: "they should all the more humbly and steadfastly pray with the Church for that grace of fidelity, which is never denied to those who seek it with a sincere heart."[37]

In particular, the Instruction *Starting Afresh from Christ* has deepened and developed reflec-

---

[35] CONGREGATION FOR INSTITUTES OF CONSECRATED LIFE AND SOCIETIES OF APOSTOLIC LIFE, Instruction *The Service of Authority and Obedience. Faciem tuam, Domine, requiram*, (11 May 2008).

[36] Cf. *Ibid.*, 30.

[37] SECOND VATICAN ECUMENICAL COUNCIL, Decree *Presbiterorum ordinis*, 16.

tion on the role of the Holy Spirit in the prayer and perseverance of the consecrated person. It urges an openness to the life-giving breath of the Holy Spirit, who becomes the author of the consecrated person's necessary perseverance.[38]

The action of the Spirit does not diminish the responsibility of consecrated persons in their life commitment. On the contrary, it is precisely their perseverance that constitutes the scope and the very means of that spiritual combat which puts all their human virtues into action, freeing them to guard the gifts of grace received and enabling them to daily renew their value in the unceasing dynamic of conversion. The Magisterium has never neglected this fundamental aspect of perseverance.

Formation: foundation of perseverance

40. The growing awareness of the importance of formation in the perseverance of consecrated persons and in their capacity to strive for it, finds its most mature and com-

---

[38] Cf. CONGREGATION FOR INSTITUTES OF CONSECRATED LIFE AND SOCIETIES OF APOSTOLIC LIFE, Instruction *Starting Afresh from Christ. A Renewed Commitment to Consecrated Life in the Third Millennium*, (19 May 2002), 10.

plete expression in the Directives *Potissimum institutioni*. Indeed, the whole document seems to be motivated by the desire to reinvigorate the quality of consecrated life and the perseverance of individual consecrated persons through appropriate formation programs. The person is called to be open to two fundamental attitudes, typical of the spiritual combat: "humility, which makes one resign oneself to the wisdom of God; and the knowledge and practice of spiritual discernment […] to be able to recognize the presence of the Spirit in all the aspects of life and of history."[39] The document recalls that in discerning God's will, the human mediation of a spiritual guide is necessary, so that the consecrated person can exercise that openness of heart which is one of the more traditional and important means of spiritual combat. This does not lessen the responsibility of each consecrated person for their own formation.[40]

---

[39] CONGREGATION FOR INSTITUTES OF CONSECRATED LIFE AND SOCIETIES OF APOSTOLIC LIFE, *Potissimum institutioni*. Directives on Formation in Religious Institutes (2 February 1990), 19.

[40] Cf. *Ibid.*, 29.

41. In this dynamism we recognize the importance of ongoing formation which urges both the consecrated person and the institute to "a continual examination regarding fidelity to the Lord; docility to His Spirit [...] constancy in the giving of self; humility in bearing with adversities."[41]

St. John Paul II in *Vita consecrata* repeatedly refers to the community dimension of the spiritual combat towards holiness. In it he invites Institutes to have courage in facing the "material and spiritual difficulties of daily life" in "complete openness to God's inspiration and to the Church's discernment."[42]

The joy of perseverance

42. The Instruction *Fraternal Life in Community* offers another qualifying component of fidelity and perseverance: joy. A fundamental gauge of fraternal life is identified in the "witness of joy" of the whole fraternity, which constitutes a further "encouragement to perseverance" for consecrated persons. "We must not

[41] *Ibid.*, 67.
[42] JOHN PAUL II, Post-Synodal Apostolic Exhortation *Vita consecrata*, (25 March 1996), 37.

forget that peace and pleasure in being together are among the signs of the Kingdom of God. The joy of living even in the midst of difficulties along the human and spiritual path and in the midst of daily annoyances is already part of the Kingdom. This joy is a fruit of the Spirit and embraces the simplicity of existence and the monotonous texture of daily life. A joyless fraternity is one that is dying out; before long, members will be tempted to seek elsewhere what they can no longer find within their own home […]."[43]

The Constitution *Lumen gentium* had already described religious families as a means to progress "spiritually rejoicing on the road of charity."[44] The subsequent Magisterium insisted on the connection between the testimony of a life of special consecration and joy, in particular through lived fraternity. "Our contemporaries – continues *Fraternal Life in Community* – want to

[43] CONGREGATION FOR INSTITUTES OF CONSECRATED LIFE AND SOCIETIES OF APOSTOLIC LIFE, Instruction *Fraternal Life in Community. Congregavit nos in unum Christi amor*, (2 February 1994), 28

[44] SECOND VATICAN ECUMENICAL COUNCIL, Dogmatic Constitution on the Church *Lumen gentium*, 43.

see in consecrated persons the joy that comes from being with the Lord,"[45] the joy of remaining faithful,[46] the fruit of the "daily loving encounter with the Word."[47]

The communities, *filled with joy and the Holy Spirit* (*Acts* 13:52), "in which solitude is overcome through concern for one another, in which communication inspires in everyone a sense of shared responsibility, and in which wounds are healed through forgiveness, and each person's commitment to communion is strengthened. The nature of the charism in communities of this kind directs their energies, sustains their fidelity and directs the apostolic work of all towards the one mission."[48] Such communities become places of evangeliza-

[45] CONGREGATION FOR INSTITUTES OF CONSECRATED LIFE AND SOCIETIES OF APOSTOLIC LIFE, Instruction *Fraternal Life in Community. Congregavit nos in unum Christi amor*, (2 February 1994), 28.

[46] Cf. CONGREGATION FOR INSTITUTES OF CONSECRATED LIFE AND SOCIETIES OF APOSTOLIC LIFE, Instruction *The Service of Authority and Obedience. Faciem tuam, Domine, requiram*, (11 May 2008), 7.

[47] *Ibid.*

[48] JOHN PAUL II, Post-Synodal Apostolic Exhortation *Vita consecrata*, (25 March 1996), 45.

tion, "places of hope and of the discovery of the Beatitudes, where love, drawing strength from prayer, the wellspring of communion, is called to become a pattern of life and source of joy."[49]

43. The Apostolic Exhortation *Vita consecrata* invites consecrated women in particular to live their own vocation "in fullness and in joy,"[50] to be "*signs of God's tender love towards the human race* and to be special witnesses to the mystery of the Church, Virgin, Bride and Mother."[51]

A specific task, also with regard to perseverance in joy, is entrusted to those who exercise the service of authority, who are invited to implore heaven, so that those entrusted to them "may always persevere with gladness in their holy purpose, unto the attainment of everlasting life."[52]

---

[49] *Ibid.,* 51.
[50] *Ibid.*, 57, 58.
[51] *Ibid.*
[52] CONGREGATION FOR INSTITUTES OF CONSECRATED LIFE AND SOCIETIES OF APOSTOLIC LIFE, Instruction *The Service of Authority and Obedience. Faciem tuam, Domine, requiram,* (11 May 2008), 30.

44. The teaching of Pope Francis is particularly attentive to joy. *Evangelii gaudium, Amoris lætitia, Gaudete et exsultate,* already through their *incipits,* all highlight a gospel demand which is fundamental in the life of the disciples: the need for joy, which is the joy of the Gospel, the joy of love, the joyful experience of communion with the Lord Jesus. Speaking to consecrated persons he continually invites them to witness joy: *"This is the beauty of consecration: it is joy, joy ...."*[53] The joy of bringing God's consolation to everyone.

Joy, for Pope Francis, is not a useless embellishment, but rather a necessity and the foundation of human life. In daily struggles, every man and woman tends to arrive and dwell in joy with the totality of their being, joy is the driving force of perseverance. "Joy is born from the gratuitousness of an encounter! [...] And the joy of the encounter with him and with his call does not lead to closing oneself in but to opening oneself up; it leads to service in the Church. St. Thomas said: *'bonum est diffusivum sui.'* Good spreads. And joy also spreads. Do not be afraid

---

[53] FRANCIS, *Meeting* with Seminarians and Novices, Vatican City, (6 July 2013).

to show the joy of having answered the Lord's call, of having responded to his choice of love and of bearing witness to his Gospel in service to the Church. And joy, true joy, is contagious; it is infectious... it impels one forward."[54]

---

[54] FRANCIS, *Authentic and coherent,* Pope Francis speaks of the beauty of consecration, [*Meeting with Seminarians and Novices*, Rome, 6 July 2013], in: *L'Osservatore Romano*, Monday-Tuesday 8-9 July 2013, CLIII (155), pg. 6.

I.
PROCESSES FOR SHARED DISCERNMENT

School of life

45. Fidelity for the perseverance of a vocation is a precious gift contained in earthen vessels (cf. *2 Cor* 4:7ff.). In this tension between the treasure received and the fragility of consecrated life, it is essential to maintain a balance that gives perspective to the process of growth of each person. It is precisely from experience that new opportunities for life can emerge which will contribute to reshaping old patterns, especially if people learn to reinterpret the conclusion of a vocational journey from a constructive motivational and affective perspective, capable of giving new meaning to everyday life. All this is possible if we look at consecrated life as a *school of life* where, in relationship with others, "we all learn to love God, to love the brothers and sisters with whom we live, and to love humanity, which is in great need of God's mercy and of fraternal solidarity."[55]

Considering departures from consecrated life as part of a *process of discernment-accompaniment* seems to be a contradiction, especially if we are dealing with people who have lived and experienced moments of difficulty and tension in their communities and Institutes. In fact, when the departure of a brother or a sister is perceived as a "liberation," something did not work well along the path of discernment. One should not arrive at the phase of final discernment through situations of exclusion or a real ostracism from the community or from the Institute: this, in fact, can fuel a sense of failure in those who leave and generate new malaise in those who remain.

46. Today a greater awareness should be given to the *educational perspective* of a Church that cares for brothers and sisters in difficulty and – when it comes to painful and difficult choic-

---

[55] CONGREGATION FOR INSTITUTES OF CONSECRATED LIFE AND SOCIETIES OF APOSTOLIC LIFE, Instruction *Fraternal Life in Community. Congregavit nos in unum Christi amor*, (2 February 1994), 25.

es – accompanies them in seeking a different path and new meanings, which can give sense to their choice of life. We have at our disposal the strengths and resources that have remained dormant. It is a matter of rediscovering them in order to reach the existential peripheries, not only in the outside world through evangelization, but also internally, within our own environments. In yielding to pessimism in the face of the phenomenon of departures, one ends up assuming an attitude of resigned passivity, or worse, to react irresponsibly, convinced that there is nothing more to do.

And yet it is precisely in these moments of painful disorientation that there is need for an accompaniment that helps to make a decision about one's life, offering "the person the support of greater trust and deeper love."[56] It is in moments of fragility, in fact, that the person feels a stronger need to rediscover the meaning of the covenant that God continues to renew without denying it, especially to those who are weak and disoriented. An educational closeness is needed which may help to retrace the path

---

[56] JOHN PAUL II, Post-Synodal Apostolic Exhortation *Vita consecrata*, (25 March 1996), 70.

of life, to the point of making choices that can also be painful "no's." Presenting the moment of departure as a process of vocational accompaniment means working together towards a discernment that continues to make sense even and above all in the most delicate and important moments of life. In this way, it is possible to face the moment of such a demanding choice with a different perspective, not of exclusion but of inclusion, respecting the diversity of choices made by the brother or sister. The moment of "crisis" can become an opportunity, a *kairòs*, not only for the individual, but for the whole community.

Working together for shared discernment

47. At the moment of initial discernment, when there were signs to be interpreted together, as well as at the moment of deciding to leave consecrated life, it is necessary to rediscover, hidden in the unfolding of events, the profound sense of a call from God and of a response from the person, in which God continues to manifest himself as the One who gives meaning to every event of human existence. It is important to also live this moment with a clear orientation and emotional support. In this sense, we need to equip ourselves with adequate tools, not only at the professional level, to be able to identify the problems, but above all in undertaking a common commitment to adequately address them. Therefore, *the practice of shared discernment* remains central to the credibility and reliability of the life and mission of consecrated men and women, in communion with the Church, particularly in the current historical context. Concluding the reflection on discernment, in the Apostolic Exhortation *Gaudete et Exsultate*, in a paragraph of particular relevance, Pope Francis summarizes the meaning of his own journey: "When, in God's presence, we examine our life's journey, no areas can be off limits. In all aspects of life, we can continue to grow and offer something greater to God, even in those areas we find most difficult. We need, though, to ask the Holy Spirit to liberate us and to expel the fear that makes us ban him from certain parts of our lives. God asks everything of us, yet he also gives everything to us. He does not want to enter our lives to cripple or diminish them, but to bring them to fulfilment. Discernment, then, is not a solipsistic self-analysis or a form of egotistical introspection, but an authentic process of leaving ourselves behind in order to approach the mystery of God, who helps us to carry out the mission to which he has called us, for the good of our brothers and sisters."[57]

Discernment and accompaniment

48. To effectively come out of ourselves towards the mystery of God is not a solitary task, but a journey in the company of young people, adults, the elderly – brothers and sisters – who set out to live together the adventure of the transforming encounter with the Lord. It is a journey towards the maturity of faith, towards becoming an adult believer (cf. *1 Cor* 13:11-12). We are called to make choices that engage our conscience as believers, to decide for ourselves and our lives in freedom and responsibility, according to the truth of God's mysterious plan, beyond the possible risks and uncertainties. This journey proceeds by stages within a formation process of personal identity, in the continuous awareness of a renewed religious or priestly identity.

[57] FRANCIS, Apostolic Exhortation *Gaudete et exsultate*, (19 March 2018), 175.

A more determined implementation of a *discernment process* at every stage and passage of consecrated life – reflecting on its meanings, objectives and modalities – involves *accompanying* the story of the perseverance of consecrated men and women in fidelity to the gift of the vocation to the *sequela Christi*. Tradition has wisely cultivated this style, which allows for a careful and effective prevention of difficulties and risks. In this scope *a process of discernment-accompaniment* for consecrated persons, which is certainly more demanding than in the past, has potential to be expressed in a new way. It is urgent to identify and face those questions which may cause concern, but which are also signs of hope. Accompaniment and discernment are inseparably united: the one occurs in the virtuous process of discernment and the other is nourished and takes the form of accompaniment.

49. Among the signs of hope we note in particular, the progressive overcoming of a mentality that tended to place the blame on those who left consecrated life, denying any responsibility to the Institute. More than fifty years after the Second Vatican Council, the experience of discernment-accompaniment communities destined for those who are going through difficult situations in their life of consecration has been developed. There has also been a growing acknowledgement of the *ministry of discernment-accompaniment* not only for those who are going through times of crisis, but also for those who, while persevering, wish to re-motivate the sense of their own fidelity. This ministry is called to face, without avoiding them, the difficult questions of consecrated men and women; it must combine experience and professionalism, in invoking the gift of *sapientia cordis*. It also implements a vigilant prevention to face even dramatic situations with a profound sense of love for the Church.

The formation of conscience

50. At the base of every discussion on discernment and accompaniment lies the moral and believing conscience. Therefore, the fundamental theme of conscience and of its formation, is set against the background of this journey. The capacity to discern is inseparable from the formation of consciences: "We have been called to form consciences, not to replace them."[58]

In today's culture, when we refer to conscience, we often like to convey an individualistic and intimate idea of self. But the centrality of the conscience "does not mean following my own ego, doing what interests me, what suits me, what I like."[59] "Conscience is the most secret core and sanctuary of a person."[60] It coincides with the personal identity of each person, with its own more or less troubled history: relationships, affections, culture of belonging. Conscience is also formed through good relationships, where one experiences that good for which it is worth dedicating one's life. In particular, first experiences are decisive for the formation of conscience, those related to family relationships, an authentic school of humanity. It is precisely in the experience of being a son or daughter, that every man and woman learns how to listen to the truth, to the good,

---

[58] FRANCIS, Post-Synodal Apostolic Exhortation *Amoris laetitia*, (19 March 2016), 37.

[59] FRANCIS, *Angelus*, Vatican City, (30 June 2013).

[60] SECOND VATICAN ECUMENICAL COUNCIL, Pastoral Constitution on the Church in the Modern World *Gaudium et spes*, 16.

to God. In these experiences of goodness, the moral conscience recognizes its profound relationship with Him, the One who speaks to the heart and helps him and her to discern, to grasp the road ahead and to remain faithful.[61] Above all it is necessary to be docile to the Word of God, ready for the surprises of the Lord who speaks.

The call of God, which echoes in goodness, requires a demanding response: as it was for the Jews in the desert (cf. *Deut* 8:2), the Christian conscience must also go through a time of trial, an arduous and difficult time. That is where what we really care about comes to light. Personal history is therefore marked by trials and, at times, by failures and disillusions that strongly challenge us to undertake a more determined formation of conscience, an essential dimension of the practice of discernment. It takes a great capacity to understand the human soul and, even more, it is a style that educates us to "God's patience and his timetable, which are never our own."[62] Fidelity to the *memoria Jesu*,

---

[61] Cf. FRANCIS, *Angelus*, Vatican City, (30 June 2013).

[62] FRANCIS, Apostolic Exhortation *Gaudete et exsultate*, (19 March 2018), 174.

lived in one's own form of life, demands this mandatory assumption of responsibility which cannot be improvised, nor delegated nor left to those who accompany irresponsibly.

In the scope of the broad theme of conscience and its relationships, we would now like to indicate some fundamental forms of discernment and accompaniment.

Self-understanding

51. Consecrated persons recognize their vocation as a gift lived with profound gratitude to the Lord: "The life that Jesus gives us – Pope Francis repeats to youth – is a love story, a life history that wants to blend with ours and sink roots in the soil of our own lives. […] The salvation that God offers us is an invitation to be part of a love story interwoven with our personal stories; it is alive and wants to be born in our midst so that we can bear fruit just as we are, wherever we are and with everyone all around us. The Lord comes there to sow and to be sown."[63] Life is understood here as a gift

---

[63] FRANCIS, *Address* during the Vigil with young people on the occasion of the XXXIV World Youth Day in Panama, Panama, (26 January 2019).

that develops the desire for a *restitutio* in view of the good of the other. It is a process of conversion that cannot overlook understanding oneself in depth. This personal self-understanding becomes the interpretative criterion of every discernment and every choice.

The initial moment of this self-understanding is a real discernment of affections. Before being an intellectual self-understanding or an effort to understand, it is a question of listening to one's own affections, to one's own feelings. Without indulging in a narcissistic self-understanding, it is rather a question of not concealing from oneself any feeling, any affection, for the fear of judging them as bad. All that is repressed, in fact, returns in other forms and becomes a poison that taints personal and community life.

Through the discernment of the affections we are able to listen to God's call, which reaches us through personal, community, social and ecclesial history, with the feelings and the desires that it arouses in us. Therefore, when this self-understanding is recognized and accepted as a vocation, it assumes the great dignity of that truth about oneself to which we cannot but be faithful. It is particularly significant that perseverance is included in the process of fulfilling one's life decision and manifests itself in faithfully preserving the truth about oneself, as it has emerged in one's personal history through lived experiences. Only such self-understanding is capable, in fact, of helping the person to take a definitive step towards a future whose contours are unknown and to persevere in a state of life which, even in difficulties, remains his or her own *choice* of life.

Gift and task

52. Personal self-understanding, in the discernment of affections, manifests itself in an existence conceived and lived as a response to God's grace which precedes and calls forth the unconditional gift of self to Him and to one's neighbor. In fact, only in a dynamic of gratuitous donation is an effective self-realization according to the Gospel of the Lord Jesus possible. The search for self-realization is a deeply felt dimension in our culture. However, in Christian discipleship it cannot be secretly desired, nor claimed, as it would void the deeper meaning of giving oneself in Christ, for Christ and with Christ. In the Christian paradox, in its profoundly human root, self-fulfillment is offered to the one who knows he must give himself or herself without reserve, even to death, because "our life on earth reaches full stature when it becomes an offering."[64] If held back, life is lost. If on the other hand, it is re-given, then it is re-found with surprising fullness. The Gospel reveals the profound truth of human life: *For whoever wishes to save his life will lose it, but whoever loses his life for my sake and that of the Gospel will save it* (*Mk* 8:35). The gift received calls us to return what has been entrusted to us, according to an authentic generative dynamic. The Paschal dimension gives the Christian, consecrated men and women, a sense of fulfillment, which enables them to live their own existence without being conditioned by the need for continuous confirmation of the choice embraced and without being dominated by the inevitable fears that arise during life. Consecrated persons are aware that, in the signs of limitations, of fragility and misery, they carry within a more intense and authentic fulfillment of their existence. The certainty of God's self-communication in history, of his humbling himself with

[64] FRANCIS, Post-Synodal Apostolic Exhortation *Christus vivit*, (25 March 2019), 254.

human frailty, nourishes the hope of being able to overcome our own limits in the persevering gift of self, without underestimating the crises and risks.

A responsible freedom

53. Existence can never cease to be lived as a vocation, since God tirelessly increases his gift. It therefore implies that the path of formation to faithful perseverance sets the conditions for a responsible freedom and for a continuous *verification* of it in a real apprenticeship of discernment. "To respond to our vocation, we need to foster and develop all that we are. This has nothing to do with inventing ourselves or creating ourselves out of nothing. It has to do with finding our true selves in the light of God and letting our lives flourish and bear fruit."[65] It is not only a question of an interior sensitivity which is attuned to the melody of the Spirit, but of constantly refining a spiritual sense which makes the free choice of the consecrated person a *vocation for humanity* – St. Paul VI in his famous speech to the United Nations defined

---

[65] *Ibid.*, 257.

the Church as an *expert in humanity*[66] – always better able to perceive the salvific event that lies behind and within one's own humanity and the daily life of one's own history.

Formation to perseverance is to be understood not as a voluntary effort centered on oneself; it aims to reawaken, to *revive* (cf. *2 Tm* 1:5) the disposition to respond to the gift received, practicing a refined interior sensitivity, of which we are not always aware of. This is the first step of discernment, a gift which God ardently desires to awaken in all believers, so that they may be "in tune" with the gift of the Spirit in their hearts.

All this should be expressed in a choice of life that highlights the human capacity to project itself over time and to make stable commitments as essential dimensions of the personal and relational identity, and of the moral coherence of one's consecrated life. Even if the life decision is made in a given time of existence, it has the characteristic of being the answer to a graced past, which at the same time opens up to a goal which guides all of life (*project*) and

[66] Cf. PAUL VI, *Address* to United Nations Organization, (4 October 1965).

becomes *traditio*, the gift of self throughout the days and works of one's life. With their decision, consecrated persons give full *assent* to their experience of God's will: their yes is a *consent* to what they are and to what God wants for them. They seal it with their free, determined agreement expressed through the rite of profession or consecration. Taken today, the decision is based on the gift experienced and anticipates the future. In this way, it precedes a future that does not yet exist and only in this horizon will the promise of God's fidelity and the value of our decision, that is its coherence, clearly appear.

Dialogue between consciences: the word and the good

54. In this perspective, discernment will have its specific place in the dialogue between consciences, and especially in the unsurpassed tradition of spiritual accompaniment, which is based on a profoundly human wisdom. Affections, in fact, need to be expressed in words. If the person remains closed in on herself, she remains a prisoner of her feelings. On the other hand, through words in dialogue, the person is able to recognize the good that is at stake in her own personal experience and which reaches into her relationship with others. In the dialogue with the other, one learns to acknowledge the good already present in the fundamental experiences of life, a decisive aspect of the moral conscience of every believer, in particular of consecrated persons.

The specific nature of the state of consecrated life requires a continuous and permanent moral formation. It is a matter of educating personal freedom, to get involved in a fruitful exchange with others and in the willingness to discover the goodness in which God himself calls us to the fullness of life. It is not sufficient to only make the doctrine and the norms known, often in a superficial or inadequate way. It is necessary to recall one's own past: where it is possible to find oneself and rediscover one's personal moral motivation. This process cannot be solely individual, but is enabled by good interpersonal relationships. The appreciation of the good takes place in the concrete situation, in the presence of one's personal choice. It is essentially a matter of taking responsibility for the formation of one's own conscience. The dialogue during spiritual accompaniment is a privileged place and time for this to occur.

Spiritual accompaniment, in fact, is a dialogue supported by the willingness to collaborate in the context of a relationship, through mutual respect, which makes it possible to listen and to propose – or re-propose – the values to be recognized, chosen, assimilated. In the apostolic exhortation *Christus vivit* Pope Francis strongly invites us to exercise the charism of listening,[67] being attentive first of all to the person: "A sign of this willingness to listen is the time we are ready to spare for others. More than the amount of time we spend, it is about making others feel that my time is their time, that they have all the time they need to say everything they want. The other person must sense that I am listening unconditionally, without being offended or shocked, tired or bored."[68]

The dialogue between consciences is a precious instrument of self-understanding, a possibility for comparison and objectivity, for discerning not only what is to be done but also what has already been done, so as to be able

---

[67] Cf. FRANCIS, Post-Synodal Apostolic Exhortation *Christus vivit*, (25 March 2019), 244.
[68] *Ibid.*, 292.

to draw from experience and from the choices which have guided and still guide our being, thinking and acting as consecrated persons. Initial and ongoing formation offer concrete possibilities aimed at promoting and safeguarding one's potential.

55. In the process of discernment the whole existence is committed to respond to the appeals that the Lord makes in the history of individuals and communities. A spiritual discernment that doesn't play a role in the moral sphere would be reduced to a spiritualistic approach, detached from any commitment in the community and in the world. A spirituality of this kind could easily fall into the legitimacy of self-referentiality, of intimism, or into the pleasure of belonging to an *élite* that considers itself superior to the rest of God's people. Pope Francis has repeatedly highlighted this temptation that is known as Gnosticism[69] denounced as a disembodied spirituality.[70] On the other hand, a moral discernment that does not

---

[69] Cf. FRANCIS, Apostolic Exhortation *Evangelii gaudium*, (24 November 2013), 94.

[70] Cf. *Ibid.*, 78, 82, 88, 89, 90, 91, 94, 180, 183, 207, 262.

take root in the spiritual experience would be reduced to an ethical decision-making or to a mere external observance, without soul and without meaning. For this reason, discernment is a moral and spiritual category, a meeting point between morality and spirituality, where the diversity of approaches to the same reality shows the anthropological and theological richness of the person called to bear fruit for the life of the world in Christ.[71]

Definitive choices

56. The need for a journey of discernment and continuous formation of conscience, as a path of responsible fidelity to the demands of the state of consecrated life, assumes not just from today, a particular relevance. "Today, a culture of the ephemeral dominates, but it is an illusion. To think that nothing can be definitive is a deceptive lie."[72] Consecrated persons find themselves living in the context of this "liquid society," in which the sense of *definitive choices*

---

[71] Cf. SECOND VATICAN ECUMENICAL COUNCIL, Decree on Priestly Training *Optatam totius*, 16.

[72] FRANCIS, Post-Synodal Apostolic Exhortation *Christus vivit*, (25 March 2019), 264.

has disappeared from language and culture. In this way it becomes difficult to propose a life commitment to men and women of our time. Today's socio-cultural context is characterized by an openness to ever new opportunities. As a consequence, *a life decision* is often postponed, if not completely removed, in the illusion of being able to reach personal fulfillment regardless of a commitment that may fully involve one's existence. In those cases, in which a definitive decision is reached, it often appears to be disturbingly fragile. Considering consecrated life in particular, the times and ways in which many consecrated men and women decide to abandon the vocation chosen as definitive, even after a long and demanding formative journey, and also after significant stages in one's experience of consecrated and priestly life – the *ordinary* use of nine years of temporary vows should not be underestimated[73] – are disturbing.

57. Living in continuous experimentation seems to be a crucial point in contemporary culture and mentality, particularly in the West:

---

[73] Cf. SACRED CONGREGATION FOR RELIGIOUS AND SECULAR INSTITUTES, *Renovationis causam*. Instruction on the Renewal of Religious Formation, (6 January 1969), 6.

one's destiny must always remain absolutely open and in one's hands, at one's disposal. As a consequence, it is not surprising that there is a diminished interest in definitive life choices. Culture and ways of thinking inevitably go in the opposite direction with respect to those who want to choose or may have chosen a definitive state of life, especially if this perspective is combined with the widespread perception of a misunderstanding of the value of the gratuitous gift of self to others. Furthermore, our social context is completely empathetic and understanding towards people who break life bonds undertaken in an irrevocable way. It cannot be concealed that this culture and mentality are also penetrating consecrated life, undermining the very concept of vocation, traditionally conceived as a bond that lasts a lifetime and which must be achieved over the course of one's life. Even in the Christian community – with respect to the recent past – expectations about the irrevocability of a vocation and the *stability* of a state of life are weaker.

Discovering new facts

58. In the eyes of some people it may seem *normal* to question the irrevocability of a life decision and for many, even stability of life. It is not supposed to be an easy or superficial decision for anyone. In the choices aimed at discovering the truth about oneself the need for accompaniment has to be addressed. Putting others in front of the *fait accompli* does not help to understand one's own difficulties. On the one hand, it is a question of engaging in a conversation with those around us or close to us, so as not to remain prisoners of a solitude that hinders freedom and responsibility: the sense of a choice of life and the perspective of a meaningful future is at stake. On the other hand, when accompanying persons in moments of crisis, not too many guarantees should be placed on the decisions to be taken, one should allow *new evidence* to be discovered in bringing to completion the gift of oneself to God and to others. If, in fact, it is important to be able to recognize one's own energies and to know the limits of one's resources, it is equally important to remember that one can dare to go beyond the perceived limit, accompanied by a fraternal, friendly, and at the same time lucid proximity, which enlightens, guides, and supports discernment in times of trial.

Opening up a path in which the person feels exposed to the underlying shadows can extinguish the desire to return to the light. One should avoid embarking on a path of self-referential management of one's own crisis which risks effecting a resigned passivity or an adaptation to one's own inconsistency or infidelity. Moreover, and not only that, it would be inconclusive to end up in a sort of spiritual wandering, looking for someone who can find solutions to our own insecurities. In the event that a decision other than the choice already made is contemplated, and supported by plausible reasons, that decision needs to be properly verified by appropriate people, times and methods. "Therefore, while clearly stating the Church's teaching, pastors are to avoid judgments that do not take into account the complexity of various situations, and they are to be attentive, by necessity, to how people experience and endure distress because of their condition."[74] Situations and problems, which are already complex

---

[74] XIV ORDINARY GENERAL ASSEMBLY OF THE SYNOD OF BISHOPS, *Relatio finalis*, (24 October 2015), 51; cit. in FRANCIS, Post-Synodal Apostolic Exhortation *Amoris laetitia*, (19 March 2016), 79.

for the human condition, cannot be weighed down by the anxiety of finding a solution as soon as possible, with the risk of not facing the real personal problems that the crisis has brought to light. The focus is therefore shifted to some criticism of one's living environment, in order to mask and cover up one's real struggle. The difficulties that can be encountered, or even suffered, do not exclude, and in some cases highlight, lifestyles showing a gradual and increasing lack of responsibility, up to a complete alienation or estrangement from one's own community.

II.
TO BE ACCOMPANIED IN TIMES OF TRIAL. THE COMMUNITY DIMENSION

Fraternity: support for perseverance

59. Without a good fraternal life, personal spiritual accompaniment is exposed to many risks. The risk is always lurking to take refuge in an intimate relationship, devoid of real community life, where we risk telling others who we would like to be but not who we really are. The perspective of common life, understood as *schola amoris*, leads us to focus on what can realistically become an opportunity for growth and change. Pope Francis invites us to *make a home*, to *create a home*, to "let prophecy take flesh and make our hours and days less cold, less indifferent and anonymous."[75] To create a home

---

[75] FRANCIS, Post-Synodal Apostolic Exhortation *Christus vivit*, (25 March 2019), 217.

is "to create bonds by simple, everyday acts that all of us can perform. A home, as we all know, demands that everyone work together. No one can be indifferent or stand apart, since each is a stone needed to build the home."[76] Communities of consecrated men and women, increasingly multi-cultural, are a formidable school of this fraternity in diversity. We are called to form communities which are human, welcoming places in which we can work around our limits. In this way, fraternity "is a valuable support to the perseverance of many.[77] Such perseverance can be achieved to the extent that certain conditions which underlie the process of interpersonal maturing are respected: that persons are aware of their own way of weaving relationships, and are co-responsible for the possibilities emerging from their mutual relationship. These two conditions have significant practical consequences on the transformative development of the group, because they help to rediscover the theological meaning of common life

---

[76] *Ibid.*

[77] CONGREGATION FOR INSTITUTES OF CONSECRATED LIFE AND SOCIETIES OF APOSTOLIC LIFE, Instruction *Fraternal Life in Community. Congregavit nos in unum Christi amor*, (2 February 1994), 57.

and are closely linked to the vocational meaning of one's existence.

A welcoming style

60. The first consequence concerns the capacity for self-transcendence, because the awareness of one's limits is a call to look beyond painful events. The experience of departures forces people to reorganize their relational style, knowing that "the unity which they must build is a unity established at the price of reconciliation."[78] This is possible on the basis of a common vision of life understood as a precious opportunity to rediscover the continuity of God's project, even in the diversity of the situations experienced.

A second consequence concerns the care that people give each other. "Within a truly fraternal community, each member has a sense of co-responsibility for the faithfulness of the others; each one contributes to a serene climate of sharing life, of understanding, and of mutual help; each is attentive to the moments of fatigue, suffering, isolation or lack of motivation

[78] *Ibid.*, 26.

in others; each offers support to those who are saddened by difficulties and trials."[79]

A third consequence, that has a more affective character, concerns the emotional experience of the group. In fact, persons can experience the transition from insecurity to a style of mutual loving appreciation if they rediscover the educational value of fraternal love. Only in this way will they be able to establish relationships where everyone feels called "to be responsible for each other's growth; to be open and available to receive the gift of the other; to be able to help and to be helped; to replace and to be replaced."[80] This authentic reciprocity, based on the example of Jesus, will help the members of every religious community and of every reality of consecrated life to create that climate of trust that encourages them to take risks in their own way of loving, rediscovering in fraternal life the meaning of a communion which strengthens the heart and conquers the fear of uncertainty. Certain that, even in this time of trial, "the love of Christ poured out in our hearts urges us to love our brothers and sis-

[79] *Ibid.*, 57.
[80] *Ibid.*, 24.

ters even to the point of taking on their weaknesses, their problems and their difficulties. In a word: even to the point of giving our very selves."[81]

To remain centered, firm in God

61. The story of each of us is woven into the narratives of the lives of brothers and sisters with whom we share a con-*vocation* which is never accidental, but left to the provident plan of God that transforms the stories of each one into a common journey in search for His face. In the daily life of consecrated men and women *bearing each other's burdens (Gal* 6:2) means accepting suffering, hardships, and discomfort. It is concretely a matter of making our own the invitation of Pope Francis of "solid grounding in the God who loves and sustains us. This source of inner strength enables us to persevere amid life's ups and downs, but also to endure hostility, betrayal and failings on the part of others. *'If God is for us, who is against us?'* (*Rm* 8:31): this is the source of the peace found in the saints. Such inner strength makes it possible

---

[81] *Ibid.*, 21.

for us, in our fast-paced, noisy and aggressive world, to give a witness of holiness through patience and constancy in doing good. It is a sign of the fidelity born of love, for those who put their faith in God (*pístis*) can also be faithful to others (*pistós*). They do not desert others in bad times; they accompany them in their anxiety and distress, even though doing so may not bring immediate satisfaction."[82]

---

[82] FRANCIS, Apostolic Exhortation *Gaudete et exsultate*, (19 March 2018), 112.

Part Three
SEPARATION FROM THE INSTITUTE
*Canonical Regulations
and the Practice of the Dicastery*

Fidelity and perseverance: rediscovering the meaning of discipline

62. Fidelity in perseverance is sometimes compromised by difficult or problematic situations – as outlined in the first part. The outcomes are not always predictable and undermine the credibility of witness or manifest a serious inconsistency with the demands of the vocation to consecrated life. Coherence is a free response motivated by love for the One who has placed his trust in us (cf. *1 Thess* 5:2). Attitudes, relationships, lifestyles, inappropriate situations or situations inconsistent with respect for religious discipline, obscure the authenticity of the response. The virtue of coherence cannot be acquired once and for all: it is supported by grace and is based on a constant and patient exercise of self-formation. Being and feeling like disciples implies accepting the *labor of love* (*1 Thess* 1:3) and its failures. If inconsistencies show the weak side of consecrated life, even more so the morally unacceptable situations.

Fidelity is tested; it is put to the test. And that testing can lead to questionable outcomes and serious disregard for the obligations of the state of consecrated life.

Inconsistencies and counter-witnesses are not just personal, almost private experiences: negative tendencies undermine the credibility of the ecclesial witness of consecrated life. The Institute cannot and must not remain a spectator in the face of situations that openly violate the fundamental norms of the *status* of consecrated persons. Tradition, universal and proper law, the practice of the Congregation for Institutes of Consecrated Life and Societies of Apostolic Life have, over time, issued guidelines, provisions, norms that are attentive to safeguarding fidelity and coherence with obligations derived from the status of a consecrated person. These obligations, if considered and lived only as duties, empty the meaning of the very vocation to the *sequela Christi*.

63. It is urgent, especially at the level of initial formation, to rediscover the meaning and implications of one of the traditions of religious: discipline. This vocabulary recalls both the assiduous exercise of apprenticeship at the school of the Gospel, the supreme Rule of consecrated persons (cf. c. 662), and the practice of conversion that ensures the effective coherence of the disciple in fidelity to the commitments (vows or other sacred bonds) taken on the day of profession or of consecration. It can be said that to have discipline, also in its traditional sense, means to be formed to coherency and not to suffer a demeaning conformism. We are disciples called to freedom (cf. *Gal* 5:13), called to make the freedom of our choice of life credible. In consecrated life the commitment to coherency is undoubtedly formed through the awareness of one's duties, an awareness that is rooted in the motivations that guide and accompany our fidelity in perseverance. The practice of one's duties that is not animated by evangelical motivations encloses consecrated life within a private horizon. This privatization, without an openness to face the hardships of daily life and the difficulties of relationships with brothers and sisters, leads to a self-referential management of one's own crises. It reaches the point of legitimating one's own decisions, detached from a loyal and serene dialogue with Superiors and, sometimes, in almost blatant marginalization or irrelevance of the rules. The service of authority is not only called to enforce the rules, but it is also their guarantor before the Institute and the Church; and above all it promotes respect for the rules in order to safeguard the faithful witness of all. All this is also accomplished through the correct application of procedures: paths to be respected not as mere functionaries, but in the awareness that they are means to safeguard the duties and the rights of all, brothers and sisters, superiors and formators.

64. Rules are precious resources for the formation in fidelity that is supported by our being together before the Lord. In this way one rediscovers fidelity in perseverance as an expression of that solidarity of vigilance which leads to bearing each other's burdens (cf. *Gal* 6:2) and feels concern for brothers and sisters as a mutual expectation in building oneself up in the Lord. From this perspective it is possible to understand the third part of the present document which organizes the legislative norms and the practice of the Dicastery in matters of absence, exclaustration, departure, and dismissal from the Institute. It also offers a contribution for a correct discernment of difficult and problematic situations in the process of accompanying those brothers and sisters who are in the process of deciding their future, and for superiors who must make decisions in their regard, in accordance with universal and proper law.

In the delicate choices of separation from the Institute of Consecrated Life or from the Society of Apostolic Life, the Church, Institutes and Societies, individual consecrated persons and communities do not cease to accompany and enlighten the disciples who, on a journey of discernment, are considering following the Master in other ways than the one embraced.

65. The procedures for separation from the Institute are divided in two groups: those *pro gratia*: absence (c. 665 § 1), transfer (c. 684), exclaustration (c. 686 § 1), the indult of departure (cc. 691 and 693); and the *disciplinary* ones: the three forms of dismissal (c. 700) for the reason mentioned in cc. 694, 695 and 696. With respect to time, the separation can be definitive or temporary. The absence referred to in c. 665 § 1 and the two forms of exclaustration mentioned in c. 686 are temporary. The indult of departure for lay members (c. 691) and the separation by dismissal (c. 700) are definitive. The transfer to another Institute (c. 684) and the indult of departure of clerical members (cc. 691 and 693) become definitive when the required conditions are fulfilled.

Absence from the religious house

66. Religious are to reside in the house where they have been legitimately assigned (cf. c. 608), and they are not to be absent from it except with the permission of the competent superior.

Lawful absence from the religious house (c. 665 § 1)

67. The permission to be absent from the religious house (or *extra domum*) entails the temporary suspension from the obligation *to live in one's own religious house observing common life*. It is up to the religious concerned to ask for the indult of absence, giving adequate reasons.

The canon distinguishes two cases:
– absence that does not exceed the duration of one year;
– absence that can last over time, and requires the permission of the Major Superior, the consent of the Council, and a just cause.

The Major Superior, with the prior consent of the Council, is authorized to grant an absence from the religious house for more than one year, for reasons of health, study or apostolate to be exercised in the name of the Institute. In such cases particular vigilance and care is required.

The absent religious remains a member of the community, bound by the vows and all the contracted obligations; retains active and passive voice, unless otherwise provided for when granted the absence; remains fully submitted to his or her legitimate Superiors and must return to the religious house if called back; must be accountable to the Superior for the money received and spent.

It is appropriate that the document granting the indult of absence explicitly states:

- the contacts that the religious must keep with the Institute;
- the exercise of rights (active and passive voice, etc.);
- the financial assistance that the Superiors may deem necessary to give.

Negligence in the fulfillment of the duties proper to the state of consecrated life or in behavior, as far as it is evident in those circumstances, or situations that go beyond the terms of the permission received, justify that the competent Superior take corrective measures against the religious.

The lawful absence from the religious house is granted for specific reasons and for a fixed period of time. When the reasons cease, the concession expires and the religious must be reintegrated into the community. Before the term of the indult expires the religious who requests it can be reinstated by the Superior; upon expiration of the indult there must be a prompt return to the community.

It is advisable for the Major Superior to inform the local Bishop of the place where the religious is to live during the absence from the Institute, if necessary, by sending a copy of the indult with the clauses contained therein. The Bishop must be informed when a religious cleric is requesting an indult of absence.

Unlawful absence from the religious house (c. 665 § 2)

68. The religious who is unlawfully absent with the intention of evading the authority of the Superiors is to be carefully sought out and helped to return and to persevere in his or her vocation.

If this action on the part of the Superiors has no effect, disciplinary measures could be adopted, not excluding, if necessary, dismissal. In fact, the unlawful absence which extends for a period of six months can be a cause of dismissal (c. 696 § 1); if it extends for twelve continuous months, the religious whose location is unknown can be dismissed *ipso facto* (c. 694 § 1, 3).[83]

Transfer to another Institute

69. The transfer to another Institute occurs when a perpetually professed member leaves his or her own Institute to be incorporated into another, without causing the interruption of the profession of religious vows.

Canon 684 regulates various cases of transfer of definitively incorporated members from one Institute to another:

---

[83] Cf. FRANCIS, Apostolic Letter issued *motu proprio Communis vita* which provides for the modification of several norms of the Code of Canon Law, (19 March 2019); CONGREGATION FOR INSTITUTES OF CONSECRATED LIFE AND SOCIETIES OF APOSTOLIC LIFE, Circular Letter on Pope Francis' *motu proprio Communis vita*, (8 September 2019).

- transfer of the perpetually professed member to another religious Institute (§ 1);
- transfer from a *sui iuris* Monastery to another Monastery of the same Institute or Federation or Confederation (§ 3);
- transfer from a religious Institute to a secular Institute or a Society of apostolic life, or from these to a religious Institute (§ 5).

The transfer can occur from one religious Institute to another, be it of pontifical right or of diocesan right. In the case of a transfer from a religious Institute to a Society of apostolic life or to a secular Institute or vice versa, an indult from the Congregation for Institutes of Consecrated Life and Societies of Apostolic Life is required (c. 684 § 5), and its instructions are to be followed.

The transfer is a *pro gratia* concession: it is to be requested by the member and cannot be imposed. The request has to be adequately motivated. The concession is subject to the evaluation and discretionary decision of the Supreme Moderator of both the Institute to which the member belongs and of the Institute to which he or she wishes to transfer, with the consent of the respective Councils.

Once consent to the transfer is obtained, the member concerned spends a probationary period of at least three years in the new Institute. The beginning and duration of the probationary period must be determined by the Supreme Moderator of the new Institute. The Supreme Moderator or the proper law will also determine the location and the activities to be carried out. During the probationary period, the member remains incorporated in the original Institute; his or her condition is similar to that of a member of temporary vows while being required to observe the regulations of the new Institute. The probationary period does not take the form of a new novitiate.

If the member refuses to make perpetual profession in the new Institute, or is not admitted by the Superiors, he or she is to return to the Institute to which he or she belongs. At the end of the probationary period, having made perpetual profession, the member is *ipso jure* incorporated into the new Institute. It is appropriate to inform the original Institute of the definitive transfer and of the incorporation of the member into the new Institute.

If the passage is requested by a clerical member who is incardinated in the original Institute or Society, at the end of the probationary period with incorporation, incardination also occurs *ipso iure* in the new Institute of consecrated life or Society of apostolic life, if these have the faculty to do so.

Exclaustration

70. Exclaustration is the absence from common life of a perpetual professed member who, while remaining a member of the Institute, is authorized by the competent Superior to reside outside the community.

Exclaustration can only be granted for grave reasons:
- for a period not exceeding three years, even if not consecutive, the Supreme Moderator is competent with the consent of the Council (c. 686 § 1);
- to extend this indult, or to grant one for more than three years, for Institutes of consecrated life and Societies of apostolic life of pontifical right is reserved to the Congregation for Institutes of Consecrated Life and Societies of Apos-

tolic Life (c. 686 § 1); or for Institutes of consecrated life and the Societies of apostolic life of diocesan right it is reserved to the diocesan Bishop in whose diocese the house to which the person is assigned is located;

- it can be imposed, at the request of the Supreme Moderator, acting with the consent of his or her Council, by the Congregation for Institutes of Consecrated Life and Societies of Apostolic Life for a member of an Institute of pontifical right or by the Bishop, in whose diocese the house to which the person is assigned is located, on a member of an Institute of diocesan right (c. 686 § 3).

For cloistered nuns the indult of exclaustration can be granted following the procedure prescribed by the Instruction *Cor Orans*, as an exception to c. 686 § 2:

- by the Major Superior, with the consent of the Council, for not more than one year (*Cor Orans*, 177);
- by the Federal President, with the consent of the Council, for a nun professed with solemn vows of a monastery of the

Federation for a period of not more than two years (*Cor Orans*, 130-131; 178-179).

Any further extension of the indult of exclaustration is reserved solely to the Congregation for Institutes of Consecrated Life and Societies of Apostolic Life (*Cor Orans*, 180).

Exclaustration requested by the member (c. 686 § 1)

71. Exclaustration can be requested by the definitively incorporated member for grave reasons, of his or her own free will, by means of a written request, and may be granted for a period not exceeding three years.

The extension of the indult of exclaustration for more than three years is reserved to the Congregation for Institutes of Consecrated Life and Societies of Apostolic Life for members of Institutes of consecrated life or Society of apostolic life of pontifical right or to the diocesan Bishop in whose diocese the house to which the person is assigned is located, for members of Institutes and Societies of diocesan right.

It is reserved to proper law or to the practice of the Institute to determine whether the three-year term is intended to be continuous or not. The Dicastery grants the Supreme Moderator the possibility of granting an indult for a new three-year term, when at least three years have passed since the previous expiration of the indult.

If exclaustration is requested by a cleric, the indult requires the prior consent of the Ordinary of the place where the cleric must reside.

Rights and obligations arising from exclaustration

72. With the granting of exclaustration, the member does not lose all the obligations and rights that belonging to the Institute of consecrated life or Society of apostolic life entails.

The juridical condition of the exclaustrated member is defined in c. 687:

- remains a member of the Institute or Society, dependent on or under the care of the competent Superiors, and – in the case of a cleric – under the care of the local Ordinary;
- lacks active and passive voice;
- is obliged to observe the proper law of the Institute in everything that is not incompatible with the new condition of his or her life.

Superiors should feel the responsibility to ensure an attentive accompaniment and, where necessary, an adequate financial support for the exclaustrated member. As far as possible, the exclaustrated member commits to provide for personal needs. If the proper law does not provide specific indications, the Moderator will proceed to define the appropriate provisions in writing.

The competent Superior will inform the Bishop when an exclaustrated lay associate resides in his diocese.

The Major Superior, remaining responsible for the exclaustrated member, may give him or her instructions, provided that they are not incompatible with his or her condition. The Major Superior as well as the diocesan Bishop may proceed with discipline and punishment towards him or her, in consideration of their respective competences; and, if necessary, can dismiss the member from the Institute according to the norm of c. 700. It is appropriate that the Major Superior and the diocesan Bishop take care of the exclaustrated members and maintain regular contact with them.

Imposed exclaustration (c. 686 § 3)

73. At the request of the supreme Moderator acting with the consent of the council, exclaustration can be imposed by the Holy See on a member of Institutes of consecrated life and Societies of apostolic life of pontifical right, or by a diocesan Bishop on a member of an Institute of diocesan right. In order to submit the request both the Superior and the Council must evaluate whether there are grave reasons, and adhere to the requirements of equity and charity.

This is a disciplinary measure adopted in exceptional cases, to protect the good of the community or of the member, when particular difficulties hinder fraternal life, prevent the exercise of the common ministry of the Institute, and create constant difficulties in apostolic action.

It is set forth for specific periods of time – three or five years – which can be extended upon expiration. In the most serious cases it is set forth *ad nutum Sanctae Sedis*, for the members of an Institute of consecrated life or a Society of apostolic life of pontifical right; *ad nutum Episcopi* for the members of an Institute of consecrated life or a Society of apostolic life of diocesan right. The conditions, eventual clauses and duration are established in the decree with which the exclaustration is set forth by the Congregation for Institutes of Consecrated Life and

Societies of Apostolic Life for the members of Institutes or Societies of apostolic life of pontifical right or by the diocesan Bishop for the members of Institutes of diocesan right.

The member must be informed of the Supreme Moderator's intention to ask for imposed exclaustration, the reasons and the evidence against him or her, with respect to the right of defense (c. 50).

The legal effects of the imposed exclaustration are similar to those of simple exclaustration (see above n. 72).

In practice, for clerics, if it is appropriate, a declaration of acceptance in the Diocese – normally in writing – by a Bishop is required. In all cases, it is advisable that the competent Major Superior takes care to inform, in writing, the Bishop of the diocese where the exclaustrated member will reside. The duty to supervise the personal and pastoral situation of the exclaustrated member belongs to the Major Superior and the local Bishop.

The Indult of Departure

74. Canons 688-693 list various cases that provide for the possibility of the definitive departure from the Institute:

- the departure of a member of temporary vows, of his or her own free will, upon the expiration of the vows (c. 688 § 1) or during the time of temporary profession (c. 688 § 2);
- the departure of a member of temporary vows at the request of the Institute (c. 689);
- the departure of a member during perpetual profession (c. 691);
- the departure of a member who is a cleric (c. 693).

The departure from the Institute always entails the loss of membership status and therefore also the relative obligations and rights.

The indult of departure for temporary professed member (c. 688 §§ 1-2)

75. The temporary professed member upon the expiration of the vows, is free to leave the Institute of consecrated life or the Society of apostolic life (c. 688 § 1).

For a grave reason, a temporary professed member may leave the Institute or the Society even during the time in which he or she is bound by vows. In this case, he or she must submit the request to the Supreme Moderator, who grants the indult, with the previous consent of the Council. The indult of departure for a temporary professed member of an Institute of diocesan right or for a member of a Monastery, as mentioned in c. 615, for validity, must be granted by the Bishop in whose diocese the house to which the person is assigned is located.

The indult of departure for temporary professed member at the request of the Institute (c. 689)

76. The member temporarily incorporated in the Institute or in the Society, for a just cause, may be excluded by the Major Superior, after consulting the Council, from making a subsequent profession or from making perpetual profession (c. 689 § 1).

The Code also provides that a reason for exclusion from the renewal of vows is a physical or psychological infirmity contracted after profession, such as to render the member unsuited to lead the life of the Institute (c. 689 § 2). To guarantee the right of the member, the assessment of the candidate's lack of suitability due to infirmity is entrusted to experts; the judgment on the suitability to lead the life of the Institute is entrusted to the Superiors.

In the event that the infirmity was due to the negligence of the Superiors, by not having guaranteed the necessary assistance and treatment, or when the infirmity was contracted because of the work performed by the member in the Institute or in the Society, the member must be admitted to renew temporary profession or to make perpetual profession.

Paragraph 3 of the canon provides that a member who becomes insane after temporary profession has the right to remain in the Institute, even though he or she is unable to make a new profession. The Institute must assume this responsibility.

Readmission of a member who lawfully left the Institute (c. 690)

77. Canon 690 authorizes the Supreme Moderator, with the previous consent of the Council, to readmit to the same Institute, without the obligation to repeat the novitiate, a member who, having made temporary or perpetual profession, has lawfully left the Institute. The norm does not apply to dismissed members, since dismissal is a different form of leaving the Institute.

Readmission without repeating the novitiate presupposes an appropriate probation period prior to temporary profession; the duration and modality of that period is determined by the Supreme Moderator.

The indult of departure for a perpetually professed member (cc. 691-692)

78. A member definitively incorporated in the Institute or the Society may request an indult of departure. This must be motivated by *very grave reasons (causas gravissimas) weighed before God*. Such a radical decision requires serious reflection:
- by the member – who has committed himself or herself to living the vocation with fidelity and perseverance –, with the help and advice of prudent and experienced persons;
- by the Major Superiors who must give instructions on the procedure for granting the indult of departure;
- by the authority competent to grant the indult.

The authorities competent to grant the indult of departure are: the Holy See for Institutes of consecrated life and Societies of apostolic life of pontifical right and Monasteries; the diocesan Bishop, in whose diocese the house to which the member is assigned is located, for Institutes of consecrated life and the Societies of apostolic life of diocesan right (c. 691 § 2).

The member presents the request for the indult of departure to the Supreme Moderator, who forwards it to the competent authority together with his or her own opinion and that of the Council (c. 691). Major Superiors of a Province or an equivalent part of the Institute (cf. c. 620), especially in internationally organized Institutes, express their own motivated opinion about granting the indult of departure to the Supreme Moderator. In fact, closer knowledge of the persons can effectively contribute to making known the real circumstances and difficulties that led the member to seek the indult.

The competent Superior first of all evaluates the validity and gravity of the reasons given by the member, for his or her good, for the good of the Institute and that of the Church. The Supreme Moderator, with the Council, is called to express an opinion on the request, which has to be forwarded to the competent authority, even if such an opinion would be contrary to the concession of the indult.

Notification of the indult of departure must be made to the member who requested it by the Superiors or directly by the Dicastery. The notification implies that the granting of the indult is brought to the attention of the person concerned, drafted in writing or communicated orally before witnesses, so that it can be proven. Upon notification, the member has the right to refuse the indult (c. 692), in which case it has no effect.

Once lawfully notified, the indult of departure from the Institute, by virtue of the law itself, carries with it the dispensation from all duties and rights arising from profession in the Institute.

The indult of departure of the cleric member (c. 693)

79. Canon 693 establishes that the indult of departure of a member who is a cleric *is not granted until he has found a Bishop who will incardinate him in his diocese or at least receive him on probation.*

In order to avoid wandering or acephalous clerics, the member who is a cleric has to find a Bishop willing to incardinate him in a pure and simple manner (*pure and simpliciter*) or to accept him experimentally (*ad experimentum*).

There is *pure et simpliciter* incardination when the Bishop is willing to incardinate the cleric in his own diocese. In this case the member who is a cleric and who wants to leave the Institute submits the request to the Supreme Moderator, who forwards it to the competent authority, accompanying it with his opinion and that of his Council, and with the written declaration of the diocesan Bishop who is willing to incardinate the cleric. If the competent authority, according to c. 691, grants the indult, the cleric is *ipso iure* incardinated in the diocese. The incardination is completed when the Bishop has received, at least in copy, the indult of departure and has issued the relative decree.

Incardination ad experimentum occurs when the Bishop is willing to receive the cleric in his own diocese for a probation period. In this case, the competent authority, according to c. 691, having received the necessary documentation, grants the cleric an indult of exclaustration, submitting it to the Bishop for the probationary period. This can last for a maximum of five years. Once the probation period has expired, the cleric can be sent back by the Bishop to his original Institute or he remains incardinated *ipso iure* to the diocese. The indult of exclaustration aims to assess the opportunity of incardination. The probationary period can be interrupted, even unilaterally, by the Bishop or by the cleric, at any time. In this case the cleric returns to the original Institute.

Reception in the diocese for incardination or for the probationary period is ordered by a decree issued by the Bishop when he receives a copy of the indult, which is notified to the member. If the Bishop issues the decree of incardination before the notification of the indult of departure, the act is invalid. In this case it will be necessary for the Bishop to issue a new decree, after the granting of the indult by the competent authority. Recently the practice has been introduced of inserting in the text of the indult a clause that asks the Bishop to forward to the Dicastery a copy of the decree of incardination or of reception on probation. As long as the decree of incardination is not issued, the cleric member continues to be juridically a member of the Institute, unless otherwise provided by proper law concerning the obligations and rights that such membership entails.

If the Bishop, having received the indult of departure, does not issue the decree of incardination, the indult of departure is ineffective and the clerical member remains a member of the Institute.

The Dicastery has also adopted the practice of defining in the text of the indult of departure granted to a cleric member a time limit within which the Bishop must issue the decree of incardination.

If the Bishop revokes his decision of incardinating or receiving the cleric, and the cleric still wishes to leave the Institute, the procedure must be restarted in order to obtain the concession of a new indult. In fact, the indult is granted for incardination or for acceptance *ad experimentum* in a particular diocese.

Particular attention must be given to the granting of an indult of departure in the course of disciplinary proceedings and pending a dismissal or appeal procedure.

DISMISSAL FROM THE INSTITUTE

80. Dismissal consists in the definitive separation of a member from the Institute of consecrated life or from the Society of apostolic life. It is imposed by the Institute or by the Society against the will of the member, and presupposes serious violations of the state of consecrated life and requires a rigorous procedure.

The Code presents four different cases:
- the *ipso facto* dismissal, which takes place by the very fact of having committed an offense (c. 694);
- the *obligatory* dismissal by decree (c. 695);
- the *discretionary* dismissal remitted to the judgment of the Institute (c. 696);
- the dismissal following an *immediate* expulsion in case of particular urgency (c. 703).

The ipso facto dismissal (c. 694)

81. The *ipso facto* dismissal (c. 694) takes place by the very fact of having committed a specific violation of canon law. In such cases the member is no longer a member of the Institute or the Society; the intervention of the competent Superior is limited to the declaration of the fact.

There are three cases of *ipso facto* dismissal:
- the notorious defection from the Catholic faith;

- contracted marriage or attempted it, even only civilly;
- a prolonged unlawful absence from the religious house lasting at least twelve consecutive months, if the religious turns out to be untraceable.[84]

The notorious defection from the Catholic Faith (c. 694 § 1, 1°)

82. The member who notoriously defects from the Catholic faith deprives himself or herself of the first requirement of admission to consecrated life. In fact, without the Catholic faith the candidate should not have been admitted to any Institute or Society.

The defection from the Catholic faith occurs in those persons who reject the truths of divine and Catholic faith, according to c. 750. Therefore, Catholic faith is lacking, in the sense determined by c. 751: the heretic who obsti-

[84] Cf. FRANCIS, Apostolic Letter Issued *motu proprio Communis vita*, with which certain norms of the Code of Canon Law are emended, (19 March 2019); CONGREGATION FOR INSTITUTES OF CONSECRATED LIFE AND SOCIETIES OF APOSTOLIC LIFE, Circular Letter on Pope Francis' *motu proprio Communis vita*, (8 September 2019).

nately denies a truth of the divine and Catholic faith, or who obstinately doubts it; the apostate who totally repudiates the Christian faith received in baptism; the schismatic who formally refuses submission to the Roman Pontiff or communion with the Hierarchy of the Church.

Defection from the Catholic faith is considered notorious when the fact is disclosed in such a way that it becomes public knowledge, by reason of the means used (press, web, public declaration), or publication of the fact.

Defection from the Catholic Church can also take the form of a true *actus formalis defectionis ab Ecclesia*, that is evidenced by: a) the interior decision to leave the Catholic Church; b) the implementation and external manifestation of that decision; c) the acceptance of that decision by the competent ecclesiastical authority.[85]

Celebrating marriage or attempting to do so, even if only civilly (c. 694 § 1, 2°)

83. The second case of *ipso facto* dismissal is the celebration of marriage or an attempt

---

[85] PONTIFICAL COUNCIL FOR LEGISLATIVE TEXTS, *Actus Formalis Defectionis ab Ecclesia Catholica*, 13 March 2006, "Communicationes," 38 (2006) 170-172.

to contract it. In fact, the member has made the vow of chastity which involves the commitment to live a celibate life and therefore the prohibition to marry.

The member who contracts marriage is dismissed from the Institute, even if there is no canonical impediment, as in the case of the temporary professed member. Marriage, by virtue of the impediment referred to in cc. 1087-1088, is an attempt, that is invalid, for clerics and religious who are bound by the public perpetual vow of chastity made in a religious Institute.

The illegitimate absence from the religious house lasting over a year (c. 694 § 1, 3°)[86]

84. Pope Francis' *motu proprio Communis vita* inserted a third reason for an *ipso facto* dismissal from the religious Institute in paragraph 1 of c. 694: a prolonged illegitimate absence from

---

[86] Cf. FRANCIS, Apostolic Letter issued *motu proprio Communis Vita* which provides for the modification of several norms of the Code of Canon Law, (19 March 2019); CONGREGATION FOR INSTITUTES OF CONSECRATED LIFE AND SOCIETIES OF APOSTOLIC LIFE, Circular Letter on Pope Francis' *motu proprio Communis Vita*, (8 September 2019).

the religious house, in accordance with c. 665 § 2, lasting at least twelve consecutive months, especially in cases in which the location of the member is unknown.

This modification offers the opportunity to find a solution to the cases of illegitimate absence of a member from the religious house, with particular reference to those who "at times cannot be located" or those who are untraceable.

The person whose home address or at least place of residence is known is considered to be available; as is the person who has communicated his or her address/place of residence. A person is to be considered unable to be contacted if one knows only: a telephone number; an e-mail address; a profile on social networks; a fictitious address.[87]

The procedure to declare the ipso facto dismissal

85. The member responsible for the acts mentioned in § 1, 1°-2° of c. 694 is dismissed

---

[87] Cf. CONGREGATION FOR INSTITUTES OF CONSECRATED LIFE AND SOCIETIES OF APOSTOLIC LIFE, Circular Letter on Pope Francis' *motu proprio Communis Vita*, (8 September 2019), 2.

ipso facto. For the dismissal to be juridically valid, the Major Superior, with the Council, must:
- promptly gather evidence of the events that have occurred;
- present them to the person concerned, in order to defend him/herself;
- issue the decree of dismissal, having reached the moral certainty of the fact.

In cases of *ipso facto* dismissals, together with the decree of dismissal, the *latae sententiae* censure of suspension for clerical members and the interdict for non-clerical members must also be declared. Likewise, the irregularity for the exercise of Holy Orders for religious clerics (c. 1044 § 1,3° and c. 1041, 3°) and the irregularity for the reception of Holy Orders for non-clerical religious (c. 1041, 3°) must be declared.

If an *ipso facto* dismissed member has been accepted and incardinated in a diocese it is necessary to postpone the suspension and obtain the dispensation from the irregularity from the Congregation for the Clergy.

If a non-clerical member who has incurred the *latae sententiae* interdict because of an attempted marriage, even if only civil, wants to celebrate a religious marriage, he must first request and obtain the dispensation from the irregularity, otherwise the marriage, even if valid, is illicit.

A copy of the decree of dismissal, for correctness, is to be sent to the religious concerned.

The procedure for declaring illegitimate absence from the religious house for over a year

86. In the *motu proprio Communis vita* the Holy Father specified, by adding § 3 of c. 694, the procedure to be followed in cases where the new case of dismissal for *illegitimate absence from the religious house for more than a year* applies.

The Major Superior has the duty to seek out the religious who is absent illegitimately and cannot be found, and in this way expressing concern for the religious so that he or she may return and persevere in his or her vocation (cf. c. 665 § 2).

If the research is unsuccessful, even if repeated over time, or if it is acknowledged that the member is intentionally not able to be contacted, it is necessary "to give legal certainty to the *de facto* situation."

To this end, the competent Superior:

- is required to produce certain proof through verifiable documentation of the research carried out, and of the attempts at contacting or communicating with the member;
- in the event of a negative outcome of the aforementioned research, the Superior proceeds to declare that the member is unable to be contacted.

The competent Superior evaluates the case with the Council and issue a declaration of inability to be contacted. This declaration is necessary for making certain the accounting of time:

- the day *a quo*, from which the religious cannot be found cannot remain uncertain, because it would make the twelve continuous month period indefinite (cf. c. 203 § 1);
- the expiration of the terms to fix the deadline of the twelve continuous months.

After twelve consecutive months, during which the situation of unavailability of the illegitimate absent member had not changed in any way, the competent Superior must proceed to the *declaration of the fact* so that the dismissal is legally valid, according to c. 694. This declaration must be confirmed by the Holy See if the Institute from which the member is dismissed is of pontifical right, or by the Bishop of the principal seat if the Institute is of diocesan right.

The new provision (c. 694 § 1, 3°) does not apply to cases prior to 10 April 2019, in other words it cannot be said to be retroactive, otherwise the Legislator should have expressly declared it (cf. c. 9).

The *motu proprio Communis Vita* called for the modification of c. 729 which regulates the life of secular institutes, because dismissal from the institute for illegitimate absence does not apply to members of such institutes.

Obligatory dismissal (c. 695 § 1)

87. Obligatory dismissal occurs when the offenses mentioned in c. 695, which refers to cc. 1397, 1398, 1395, are committed:
- murder, kidnapping, abduction, mutilation and gravely wounding a person (c. 1397);
- procuring a completed abortion (c. 1398);

- concubinage and persistent scandal in another external sin against the sixth commandment (c. 1395).

The cases referred to in c. 1395 are crimes only if committed by religious or diocesan clerics.

The crime of murder, kidnapping and abduction, mutilation and grave wounding of a person (c. 1397)

88. Canon 1397 specifies some crimes deliberately committed against the life and freedom of a person. For these crimes the offender is punished with the penalties prescribed in c. 1336, in proportion to the gravity of the offense.

If the murder is committed against the person of the Roman Pontiff or against a consecrated Bishop or against a cleric or a religious the penalty is established in c. 1370:

- for the murder of the Roman Pontiff: excommunication *latae sententiae*, with the addition of other penalties, not excluding dismissal from the clerical state, if the offender is a cleric;

- for the murder of a consecrated Bishop: interdict *latae sententiae* and, if the offender is a cleric, he also incurs the suspension *latae sententiae*;
- for the murder of a cleric or a religious: a just penalty, *ferendae sententiae*.

The crime of abortion (c. 1398)

89. Abortion is a crime for every believer, cleric, religious or non-religious, consecrated or not consecrated. Canon 1398 considers the voluntary interruption of pregnancy as a crime, either by expelling the immature fetus or by killing the fetus in any way and at any time once conception is procured.[88]

Abortion is punished with the excommunication *latae sententiae*, in which both the woman who voluntarily procures it and all those who, physically or morally, have cooperated directly and effectively.[89]

---

[88] PONTIFICIAE COMMISSIONIS CODICIS IURIS CANONICI AUTHENTICE INTERPRETANDO, Responsio *Utrum abortus*, de abortu (c. 1398), 23 maii 1988, in *AAS* 81 (1989) 388.

[89] *Catechism of the Catholic Church*, nn. 2270-2273; CONGREGATION FOR THE DOCTRINE OF FAITH, Clarifica-

Concubinage or another external sin against the sixth commandment of the Decalogue (c. 1395 § 1)

90. Paragraph 1 of c. 1395 considers the case of the cleric in the state of concubinage or in a situation of permanent scandal in another external sin against the sixth commandment of the Decalogue.

Concubinage means: relationship *more uxorio*, characterized by a certain stability, even without living together under the same roof.

Another sin against the sixth commandment, different from concubinage, concerns the case of a cleric who continues in some other external sin which causes scandal.

The penalty established for these crimes is the suspension *ferendae sententiae*; other penalties can be added to that, not excluding dismissal from the clerical state, if the cleric, after having been warned, persists in the offense.

The cleric living in concubinage or who continues in some other external sin against the sixth precept of the Decalogue cannot lawfully

tion on procured abortion, 11 July 2009, in *L'Osservatore Romano*, Anno CXLIX n. 157 (11 July 2009), p. 7.

celebrate the Eucharist (c. 900 § 2), nor can he receive holy communion (c. 915).

Other crimes contra sextum (c. 1395 § 2)

91. Paragraph 2 of c. 1395 examines other crimes committed against the sixth commandment:
- by force, that is when the person's freedom is taken away;
- or by threats, instilling fear;
- publicly;
- or with a minor below the age of 16 years, if the religious is not a cleric;
- or, with a minor below the age of 18 years if the religious is a cleric.[90]

For such crimes the Code establishes the Superior's obligation to consider the offense, evaluate it and make a discretionary decision on the need to proceed with the dismissal.

In the case of abuse of a minor under the age of 18 years, to which are equated those who

[90] JOHN PAUL II, Apostolic Letter issued *motu proprio Sacramentorum sanctitatis tutela*, Roma (30 April 2001).

habitually have an imperfect use of reason,[91] if the accused religious is a cleric, the exclusive jurisdiction lies with the Supreme Tribunal of the Congregation for the Doctrine of the Faith, according to the *motu proprio Sacramentorum sanctitatis tutela*.[92] Like all other crimes included therein, the statute of limitations is twenty years and, for the sole case of abuse of a minor under the age of 18 years, it becomes effective from the moment the child reaches the age of 18 years.

When it comes to a non-clerical member, the jurisdiction lies with the Congregation for Institutes of Consecrated Life and Societies of Apostolic Life.

In cases covered by § 2 of c. 1395, the Superior must proceed with the dismissal, unless he or she estimates it opportune to provide for the member's amendment in another way, for the restoration of justice and the reparation of the scandal (c. 695, § 1). In the above cases, the

---

[91] CONGREGATIO PRO DOCTRINA FIDEI, *Normae de delictis Congregationi pro Doctrina Fidei reservatis seu Normae de delictis contra fidem necnon de gravioribus delictis*, 21 maggio 2010, *AAS* 102 (2010) 419-434, art. 6, § 1, 1°.

[92] JOHN PAUL II, Apostolic Letter issued *motu proprio Sacramentorum sanctitatis tutela*, Roma (30 April 2001).

obligation concerns the duty of the Major Superior to initiate the process of dismissal, observing the procedure prescribed in the Code (c. 695, § 2).

The procedure for obligatory dismissal (c. 695 § 2)

92. The competence to proceed in cases of obligatory dismissal lies with the Major Superior (c. 620), assisted by the notary. Disciplinary action is not subject to time limits as are criminal actions (c. 1362). Therefore, even if the crime is prescribed, disciplinary action, by reason of c. 695 § 1, must always be instructed.

Upon receiving a complaint or the news of actions likely to be criminal, the competent Superior:

- collects the evidence concerning the facts and the imputability of the offense;
- if he or she reaches moral certainty about the truth of the facts and their imputability for malice or negligence, he or she notifies the member to be dismissed of the accusation and the evidence, giving him the possibility to defend himself;
- transmits all acts to the Supreme Moderator.

The Major Superior can adopt the procedure envisaged for the preliminary investigation referred to in cc. 1717-1719.

The Supreme Moderator, with the Council, further evaluates the accusations, the evidence, the defense and, by collegial vote, decides whether to dismiss the member. For validity, the Council must be complete or consist of at least four members. The vote is always collegial, whether it is decided in favor or against the dismissal, and therefore it must consist of at least five votes. Unanimity is not required to decide on the dismissal: an absolute majority is sufficient; and the vote must be secret (c. 699 § 1).

If, however, the Major Superior ascertains the accusations unfounded, he must dismiss the case.

Discretionary dismissal (c. 696 § 1)

93. Canon 696 leaves to the judgment of the Major Superior the dismissal of a member for causes other than those provided for *ipso facto* and obligatory dismissal. Given the seriousness of the dismissal measure, the Code requires that these causes be *grave, external, imputable and juridically proven*. Canon 696 § 1 provides for certain types of improper conduct which, although they are not criminal offenses, are in any case significantly contrary to the discipline of consecrated life. The Code presents a non-exhaustive list of these causes:

- habitual neglect of the obligations of consecrated life;
- repeated violations of the sacred bonds;
- stubborn disobedience to the legitimate prescripts of Superiors in a grave matter;
- grave scandal arising from the culpable behavior of the member;
- stubborn upholding or diffusion of doctrines condemned by the Magisterium of the Church;
- public adherence to ideologies infected by materialism or atheism;
- the illegitimate absence from the religious house, if it extends for a period of six months, with the intention of withdrawing from the authority of Superiors (c. 665, § 2);
- other causes of similar gravity which the proper law of the Institute may determine.

A member in temporary vows can be dismissed for grave reasons – even less grave than those mentioned (c. 696, § 1) –, external, imputable and juridically proven, as determined in the Institute's proper law (c. 696, § 2).

The cases occurring most frequently are: stubborn disobedience and illegitimate absence.

For the purposes of dismissal, disobedience is juridically valid if the member acts in opposition to a provision on serious matters, given by the Superior in accordance with universal and proper law, or at least not in conflict with it.

The procedure for discretionary dismissal (cc. 697-700)

94. In order to protect the rights of individuals and the demands of justice, canons 697-700 carefully determine the procedure to be followed in the event of a dismissal.

Unlike the process of obligatory dismissal (c. 695 § 2), in the cases referred to in c. 696 § 1, the competent Major Superior is obligated to hear the opinion of the Council before beginning the process (c. 697). The Council, which must be validly and legitimately convened, expresses its opinion, not necessarily unanimously, on the opportunity of initiating the process and the rationale for starting it.

When the Major Superior considers that one of the cases mentioned in c. 696 which could justify the dismissal has occurred, he or she first of all proceeds to recall the religious to the fulfillment of his or her duties, not excluding recourse to canonical sanctions. If this is futile, the Major Superior:

– consults the Council on the opportunity to initiate the dismissal process, drawing up a specific "extract of meeting minutes;"
– having heard the Council, if it is judged necessary to proceed with the dismissal, collects and integrates all the evidence of the imputable facts;
– in the event that he or she wants to obtain the return of an unlawfully absent religious he or she must provide a formal precept of obedience in writing; the unlawfully absent religious is to be notified by letter sent by registered mail with acknowledgment of receipt, or orally in front of two witnesses. In the aforementioned document the Major Superior will clearly indicate a reasonable date for returning to a specific community. Also, for other reasons the Major Superior

must formally and explicitly inform the member that if he or she does not renounce the improper behavior, the dismissal process will be carried out;
- proceeds to a first canonical warning, notified in writing or before two witnesses or by edict if the member cannot be located; the warning must explicitly contain the threat of dismissal, in the case of incorrigibility, and must clearly indicate what the member must do or omit in order to avoid it; it must clearly and precisely express the fact for which he or she is accused, giving the member every opportunity for self-defense, within at least fifteen days from the notification of the warning;
- if the first warning has no effect, a second warning is to be given after an interval of at least fifteen days after receiving it, using the same procedure;
- after at least fifteen days from the date of notification of the second warning, if this is also ineffectual, convenes the Council and – by secret vote – after judging whether there is sufficient proof of incorrigibility and that the defense by the

member is insufficient, must proceed to send the request of dismissal to the Supreme Moderator;
- forwards to the Supreme Moderator all the documents, signed by a notary, together with the signed replies of the member.

There must be conclusive proof for all of the notifications.

The member always retains the right to communicate personally with the Supreme Moderator and directly expose the arguments in his or her own defense (c. 698).

The Supreme Moderator, having received the acts from the competent Major Superior, convenes the Council, which for validity must comprise at least four members, and proceeds in a collegial fashion, that is:
- weighs the evidence, the arguments, the warnings, the legitimacy of the procedure, the defense of the accused, his incorrigibility;
- having ascertained the existence of all the aforementioned elements, the college decides by secret ballot whether to proceed to the dismissal (c. 119). Since this is a collegial action, the Supreme

Moderator can settle any parity with a second vote. The secretary or notary draws up minutes with the reasons for the decision;
- if the decision favors dismissal, the Supreme Moderator issues the decree of dismissal, which for validity must express at least in summary form the reasons in law and in fact (c. 699, § 1);
- forward the decree of dismissal to the Congregation for Institutes of Consecrated Life and Societies of Apostolic Life, together with all the acts.

If it is a Monastery *sui iuris*, according to c. 615, the Superior of the Monastery, after having fulfilled his or her duties as Major Superior, will forward everything to the diocesan Bishop.

To enter into force the decree of the Supreme Moderator (c. 700) must be confirmed:
- by the Congregation for Institutes of Consecrated Life and Societies of Apostolic Life, for a member of an Institute of consecrated life or of a Society of apostolic life of pontifical right;
- by the Bishop in whose diocese the house to which the dismissed member

belongs is located, if it is an Institute of consecrated life or a Society of apostolic life of diocesan right.

The examination of the decree and the accompanying acts allows the Holy See or the Bishop to verify the procedure followed and the reasons given.

For *sui iuris* Monasteries of pontifical right the dismissal decided by the Bishop, like that decided by the Supreme Moderator on which the Monastery depends, requires the confirmation of the Holy See.

Canonical warnings

95. Care should be used in the formal editing of canonical warnings, which must be clear and brief; their content must be the same for the first and for the second. The warnings must include at least three elements:

- the legal grounds, that is the citation of the legislative code upon which it is based;
- a brief statement of the facts, that is what the member did or failed to do;
- a clear and determined statement about what the member must or must not do.

The text of the warnings must specify that the member has the right to present a defense to the Major Superior who initiated the process, or directly to the Supreme Moderator, if considered more appropriate.

Warnings are to be notified and therefore it is necessary that there be proof that the member has received them. Notification methods may differ; the choice belongs to the Major Superior, after having evaluated the circumstances.

There should be an interval of at least 15 days between the sending of one warning and of the next one, or of a different period established in the warning, within which to comply with the precept contained therein. That period can exceed the 15 days but cannot be shorter, it starts from the day of notification of the warning, that is from when the member received the warning, and not from when it was issued by the Major Superior, nor from when it was sent.

Notification of the decree of dismissal

96. The decree of dismissal once confirmed by the Congregation for Institutes of Consecrated Life and Societies of Apostolic Life, or by the diocesan Bishop, must be made known to the person concerned by the competent Superior by registered letter with acknowledgment of receipt, or personally, in the presence of two witnesses. For validity, the decree must indicate the right of the dismissed member to have recourse to the competent authority, within ten days of receiving the notification.

For the dismissal to be effective, the competent Superior must give notification of the original decree and the rescript of confirmation granted by the Dicastery or by the Bishop, in original or at least in certified copy.

Upon receipt of the notification, the member who does not intend to accept it:

- before proposing recourse, must request the revocation or emendation of the decree in writing from its author. Once this petition is made, by that very fact suspension of the execution of the decree is also understood to be requested (c. 1734 § 1)
- if he or she is a member of an Institute of consecrated life or a Society of apostolic life of pontifical right, he can have recourse in first instance to the Congregation for Institutes of Consecrated Life

and Societies of Apostolic Life, in second instance to the Supreme Tribunal of the Apostolic Signatura, and in third instance to the same Supreme Tribunal;
- if he or she is a member of an Institute of consecrated life or a Society of apostolic life of diocesan right, he can have recourse in first instance to the Bishop who confirmed the decree, in second instance to the Congregation for Institutes of Consecrated Life and Societies of Apostolic Life, and in third instance to the Supreme Tribunal of the Apostolic Signatura.

It is sufficient that the dismissed member, within 10 days from the notification of the decree, expresses in writing – even briefly – to an ecclesiastical authority his or her willingness to have recourse. Those receiving the recourse must forward it to the competent authority to process it and establish a time period within which the applicant must submit the complete appeal, accompanied by the reasons and evidence.

During the time of the recourse the juridical effects of the dismissal are suspended.

Effects of dismissal (c. 701)

97. With legitimate dismissal, both the vows and the rights and duties deriving from profession automatically cease.

If the dismissed member is a deacon or a presbyter, he retains clerical status but by virtue of the dismissal he cannot exercise sacred orders until he finds a Bishop who will receive him in his diocese to incardinate him or for a probationary period (c. 693), or who will at least allow him to exercise sacred orders (c. 701).

Support given to the dismissed or dispensed member (c. 702)

98. The dispensed or dismissed member cannot claim any right from the Institute of consecrated life or from the Society of apostolic life of which he or she was a member (c. 702 § 1). The work provided in favor of the Institute or of the Society and the fruit of the work offered to the Institute or to the Society during his or her stay in them (cf. c. 668 § 3), do not confer on a member, who left voluntarily or is dismissed, any right to receive compensation. Indeed, members have pledged to offer their work as a gratuitous expression of love and charity towards their brothers and sisters, both within the Institute or Society, and externally.

The Institute of consecrated life or the Society of apostolic life, on the other hand, *are to show equity and evangelical charity* towards the member who separates from it either by leaving or by dismissal. Equity is commensurate with the personal situation and circumstances as well as the real possibilities of the Institute; charity is commensurate with the actual needs of the member, at least for the period immediately after leaving or after dismissal, until he or she can provide for himself or herself in another way, as well as to the possibilities of the Institute.

Conclusion
"Remain in my love" (*Jn* 15:9)

The strength of a vocation

99. Today, faced with the loss of perseverance of so many brothers and sisters who had generously taken the path of discipleship, we can become harsh judges, highlighting flaws and fragility which have not been addressed in the right way, either for personal reasons or institutional reasons or collective responsibilities. Those who leave must seriously question themselves about the reasons for the failure of their own vocational choice. Those who remain must also seriously question themselves about the reason to *remain* and the consistent style of their decision and about possible implications in causes for departure and diminishing perseverance among those who have left. We are all mutually responsible and *stewards* (cf. *Gn* 4:9) of our brothers and sisters, especially the weakest ones, because we are "united in Christ as a distinctive family" and the bonds of fraternity must be cultivated with loyalty in order to foster "mutual support for all in fulfilling the vocation of each."[93]

100. *Remain in my love* (*Jn* 15: 9): is the request that Jesus makes to his disciples during

---

[93] c. 602.

the Last Supper. *Remain*: "There is where the strength of a consecrated vocation is found."[94] This imperative is also a gift, the offering of the fundamental truth that allows one to "remain in vital communion with Christ."[95] This is true for the disciples of both yesterday and today, in particular for consecrated men and women who face the challenge of living in highly secularized environments, running the risk of losing the fervor and joy of their donation to Christ and the Church.

A testament of love

101. The Fourth Gospel places the invitation to remain in love at a particular moment in the life of Jesus: that which precedes the Passion. As he advances towards the *hour* foretold at Cana (cf. *Jn* 2:4), towards the fulfillment of his mission, the surrender of his life, the evangelist John focuses on the story of the last meal with his own to bring to light treasures which

[94] FRANCIS, *The Strength of a Vocation. Consecrated Life Today. A Conversation with Fernando Prado*, CMF, United States Conference of Catholic Bishops, Washington DC, 2018, pg. 35

[95] FRANCIS, *Regina Coeli*, Vatican City, (3 May 2015).

illuminate his identity as the Son of God and that of his disciples. Sitting at table, in an atmosphere of intimacy and sharing, Jesus opens his heart to transmit to his disciples – in the form of a *testament* – that love that he not only has and gives, but the love that he himself is.

Disciples destined to bear fruit

102. In the long farewell discourse which Jesus addresses to his disciples (*Jn* 13:31-17:26), Jesus manifests his will to communicate to them the love of the Father, a love capable of making everything fruitful, ensuring authentic generativity. His life is so full of the Father's love that Jesus wants nothing more than to pour it into the disciples' life. For this reason, in *Jn* 15:1-17, he asks his disciples to be rooted in his love, to immerse themselves in the filial atmosphere of his existence and to live in the incessant exchange of love that exists between Him and the Father.

103. In *Jn* 15:9-17 the allegory of the previous verses is explained and the secret of the disciples' fruitfulness is revealed: love. This becomes the *habitat* of existence to the extent that it is received from the source that is Christ. At the origin of the love that Jesus has for his disciples there is the love with which he is loved by his Father: *as the Father has loved me, so have I loved you* (*Jn* 15:9). Jesus reveals to his disciples that the source of the love he has for them is the love that the Father has for him.

To remain is to persevere

104. The expression to *remain in*, repeated several times in the Gospel of John,[96] allows, therefore, for an understanding of the symbolism of the *vine – vinedresser – branch – fruit* in the perspective of perseverance. Christ teaches us that "to live in the flow of God's love, to take up permanent residence there, is the condition to ensure that our love does not lose its ardor and boldness."[97]

To avoid the drama of the abandonment of discipleship or the possible sterility of the vocation, the disciples are urged to *remain*. This verb, so dear to the fourth gospel, refers to the constant desire and commitment to correspond to the love of the covenant and to adhere to the model of Christ.

---

[96] Cf. *Jn* 8:31; 14:10; 15:4[x2],5,6,7,9,10.
[97] FRANCIS, *Regina Coeli*, Vatican City, (6 May 2018).

What allows us to remain in Jesus' love is the observance of his commandments (*Jn* 15:10), the docile listening to his Word. This listening changes the hearts of the disciples: from a heart of *servants* it makes it a heart of *friends*. It makes them friends in an authentic and lasting relationship with Jesus (*Jn* 15:13-15).

That your joy may be full

105. The mission of the baptized consists precisely in making the divine gifts in us bear fruit for the benefit of all, in the way Jesus gave himself for his friends and *for the life of the world* (*Jn* 6:51). To *remain in love*, is also to understand that "love is service,"[98] it is taking care of others. Only the love of the Father revealed in Jesus has the power to snatch the disciples from the risk of escaping and derailment and to destine them to fruitfulness: *I commissioned you to go out and to bear fruit and your fruit will last* (*Jn* 15:16).

Fidelity in the mutual immanence between the vine and the branches, that is, between the Master and the disciples, is a gift of mutual

---

[98] FRANCIS, *Homily* on the occasion of the pastoral visit to the Roman Parish of the Blessed Sacrament in Tor de' Schiavi, Rome, (6 May 2018).

trust, but it must be exercised in prolonged perseverance in the times and seasons of life. We all *need perseverance* (*Heb* 10:36), which is at the same time to *keep our gaze fixed on Jesus who leads us in our faith and brings it to perfection* (*Heb* 12:2), but also acting with frankness and creativity in going through moments of darkness and in supporting one another, to *make straight paths for your feet* (cf. *Heb* 12:13).

It is not possible to circumvent the trial, but it is necessary to go through it with love, strengthening more strongly the union with Christ. Thus, trial becomes a further apprenticeship of the gift of self in order to stop living only for oneself (cf. *Rm* 14:7) and to reestablish a stable friendship with Christ and with others that brings forth fruit and *complete joy* (*Jn* 15:11).

Mary, faithful and persevering woman

106. To Mary, our Mother, the faithful woman who desires the fidelity of her sons and daughters in the response of love and total dedication to Christ, we entrust all consecrated men and women, so that they may persevere in the joy of the vocation received.

Mary, faithful woman,
you were docile in welcoming
the Spirit of truth that proceeds from the Father,
through your Son Jesus,
teach us to preserve the gift of a vocation
and to rediscover its vitality day by day.

We look to you,
to contemplate God's work
which renews our ability to love
and heals our wounded fidelity.

We look to you,
persevering in following,
watchful guardian and lover of the Word
(cf. *Lk* 2:19; 2:51b),
to contemplate the blessedness
of those who through fidelity bear much fruit.

We look to you,
persevering at the foot of the cross
(cf. *Jn* 19:25)
to stand beside the infinite crosses of the world,
where Christ is still crucified
in the poor and the abandoned,
to bring comfort and support.

We look to you
persevering with the Apostles
in prayer (cf. *Acts* 1:12-14),
to burn with the Love that never goes out,
to walk in joy
and to face defeats and disappointments
without anxiety.

Mary, faithful woman, pray for us.
obtain for us from your Son and our Redeemer
a living and loving faith,
a humble and industrious charity,
to live the gift of fidelity
in perseverance,
humble and joyful seal of hope.
Amen.

Vatican City, 2 February 2020
Feast of the Presentation of the Lord

João Braz Card. de Aviz
Prefect

✠ José Rodríguez Carballo, O.F.M.
Archbishop Secretary

INDEX

Introduction 3

Part One
Gazing and Listening

I. THE PHENOMENON OF DEPARTURES: SOME
   CRITICAL ISSUES 15
   A phenomenon that questions us 15
   Forms of discomfort. 17
   A watchful gaze and attentive listening . . . 18
   Crisis of the Institutes: uncertainty and disorientation 20
   An obscure attraction 21
   The inadequate evaluation of the difficulties. . . 23

II. INSTANCES TO BE INTERPRETED AND DYNAMICS
    TO BE CONVERTED 25
    Identity building processes. 25
    Faith: an illusory light. 27
    *The way of understanding and living consecrated
    celibacy* 28
    A liquid fidelity 30
    The meaning of a rule-oriented bond 31
    Relationship with time and space 32
    Difficult interpersonal and community relationships 33
    The experience of solitude. 34

Tension between community and mission	35
Management of the digital world	36
Relationship with power and possession	38

Part Two
Enkindling awareness

I. FIDELITY AND PERSEVERANCE 43
Memoria Dei 43
God is the faithful One 44
Christ, iconic image of fidelity 45
Fidelity is nourished by encounters 48
To persevere: memory and hope 49
To persevere in fidelity 52
Total and exclusive love 53
Mary model of perseverance 56
A path of increasing fidelity 57
Perseverance on the path of holiness 60
Fraternal life: a place of perseverance 62
Co-responsible for the fidelity of brothers and sisters 64
Persevering in prayer 67
Formation: foundation of perseverance 68
The joy of perseverance 70

II. PROCESSES FOR SHARED DISCERNMENT 77
School of life 77
Working together for shared discernment 80

Discernment and accompaniment	82
The formation of conscience	84
Self-understanding	87
Gift and task	89
A responsible freedom	91
Dialogue between consciences: the word and the good	93
Definitive choices	97
Discovering new facts	99

III. TO BE ACCOMPANIED IN TIMES OF TRIAL.
THE COMMUNITY DIMENSION 103
   Fraternity: support for perseverance. 103
   A welcoming style 105
   To remain centered, firm in God 107

Part Three

Separation from the Institute

Canonical Regulations and the Practice of the Dicastery

Fidelity and perseverance: rediscovering the meaning of discipline	111
ABSENCE FROM THE RELIGIOUS HOUSE	116
Lawful absence from the religious house (c. 665 § 1)	116
Unlawful absence from the religious house (c. 665 § 2)	118
Transfer to another Institute	119
Exclaustration	122
Exclaustration requested by the member (c. 686 § 1)	124

179

Rights and obligations arising from exclaustration	125
Imposed exclaustration (c. 686 § 3)	126
THE INDULT OF DEPARTURE	128
The indult of departure for temporary professed member (c. 688 §§ 1-2)	129
The indult of departure for temporary professed member at the request of the Institute (c. 689)	130
Readmission of a member who lawfully left the Institute (c. 690)	131
The indult of departure for a perpetually professed member (cc. 691-692)	132
The indult of departure of the cleric member (c. 693)	134
DISMISSAL FROM THE INSTITUTE	137
The ipso facto dismissal (c. 694)	138
The notorious defection from Catholic Faith (c. 694 § 1, 1°)	139
Celebrating marriage or attempting to do so, even if only civilly (c. 694 § 1, 2°) . .	140
The illegitimate absence from the religious house lasting over a year (c. 694 § 1, 3°).	141
The procedure to declare the ipso facto dismissal	142
The procedure for declaring illegitimate absence from the religious house for over a year	144
Obligatory dismissal (c. 695 § 1)	146

The crime of murder, kidnapping and abduction, mutilation and grave wounding of a person (c. 1397) 147
The crime of abortion (c. 1398). . . . 148
Concubinage or another external sin against the sixth commandment of the Decalogue (c. 1395 § 1) 149
Other crimes contra sextum (c. 1395 § 2) 150
The procedure for obligatory dismissal (c. 695 § 2) 152
Discretionary dismissal (c. 696 § 1) 153
The procedure for discretionary dismissal (cc. 697-700). 155
Canonical warnings 160
Notification of the decree of dismissal. . 161
Effects of dismissal (c. 701) 164
Support given to the dismissed or dispensed member (c. 702) 164

Conclusion
Remain in my love (*Jn* 15:9)

The strength of a vocation. 169
A testament of love. 170
Disciples destined to bear fruit 171
To remain is to persevere 172
That your joy may be full 173
Mary, faithful and persevering woman. . . 174

CPSIA information can be obtained
at www.ICGtesting.com
Printed in the USA
BVHW031203191021
619309BV00005B/62